# Vegetable Gardening

**By Fred Bonnie**
**and the Editors of**
***The Progressive Farmer***
**and *Southern Living* Magazines**

**GALAHAD BOOKS · NEW YORK CITY**

Published by arrangement with Oxmoor House, Inc.
ISBN: 0-88365-344-3

Library of Congress Catalog Number: 75-32259

Manufactured in the United States of America

First Printing 1976

## Vegetable Gardening

Editor: Grace Hodges
Cover Photograph: Taylor Lewis
Illustrations: Ralph Mark
Photographs: Jack Goodson, Joe Benton, H.C. Thompson,
    and John Grunke

# Contents

# Introduction

Vegetable gardening is like cooking spaghetti sauce; everyone has his own recipe. Both are easy, affording the beginner as well as the veteran a chance at success. And for both the novice gardener and the novice cook, skill is increased with each attempt.

There are no great mysteries to growing a fine vegetable garden. Primitive man, with his simple mind and simple tools, fed himself amply from the vegetable garden and the meat he hunted. Today's tools and techniques make vegetable gardening far easier than it was 5,000 years ago; so easy, in fact, that gardening is now considered primarily a recreational activity. Gardening is far more, however.

Gardening provides exercise, education, ecological awareness, satisfaction, inner peace, nutritious food, tastier food, and food you may not be able to find at the supermarket. So important has vegetable gardening become to educators that many schools across the country, both private and public, now offer courses in vegetable gardening. A new sense of community pride has been awakened in the community gardening projects throughout the United States and Canada. Churches, schools, corporations, public parks, and private individuals have offered land on which landless apartment dwellers are now able to grow vegetable gardens, a phenomenon reminiscent of the Victory Gardens of World War II days when backyard gardening was viewed as patriotic.

We hope in this book to provide a basic, simple garden recipe on which the gardener can build and improvise as he gains knowledge and experience. Photographs and how-to illustrations are provided throughout to guide even the rank novice in performing such essential gardening activities as planting, fertilizing, watering, weeding, harvesting, and warding off insects and other pests.

The experienced gardener will find *Vegetable Gardening* an invaluable reference for growing new vegetables and herbs, selecting the best varieties, and diagnosing unfamiliar growth problems.

All gardeners will find useful such features as the detailed table of contents, glossary, index, pesticide charts, and the appendix listing of the 50 state Agricultural Extension Services through which one may obtain up-to-the-minute information to answer gardening questions.

# Planning and Preparation

## Planning the Garden

There are five main things to consider in planning: 1) How much of each vegetable to grow, 2) Which varieties are best, 3) When to plant for optimum production and continuous supply, 4) What tools and other supplies are needed (or are in need of repair), 5) Which insects and diseases may attack your plants.

### HOW MUCH TO GROW

Make spring plantings large enough to compensate for losses due to weather, pests, or weeds. You will then be able to replant, if necessary, in plenty of time to produce a crop before fall frost. Take into account how much you intend to can or freeze. The following chart will help you determine how much seed to buy and which vegetables will provide the most nutrition.

### EASY VEGETABLES FOR BEGINNING GARDENERS

Vegetable gardening affords one an excellent opportunity to try many foods that are hard to find in the supermarket. The beginning gardener is likely to want to try everything the first year. This is exciting and adventurous and, frankly, a lot of work. Even the experienced gardener loses some of his crops, so the beginner should be prepared to accept some failures, despite his most attentive efforts. Some crops are a good deal easier to grow than others. Include some of the following in your garden so that when your celery seed fails to germinate, it won't mean the end of your garden:

| | |
|---|---|
| Carrots | Turnips |
| Beets | Collards |
| Beans (bush, pole) | Black-eyed peas |
| Lettuce | English peas |
| Radishes | Squash |
| Okra | Chinese cabbage |
| Mustard greens | |

### SELECTING SEED AND VARIETIES

Select vegetable varieties on the basis of their resistance to insects and diseases and their adaptability to your climate. Check with the office of the county Agricultural Extension Agent, whose telephone number is listed in your directory under "Government, County," or write your state's Extension Service (see addresses in Appendix) to find out which varieties perform best in your area.

Test newly released varieties on a small scale alongside the ones you've been growing to compare them. Depend on those varieties which have proven their value.

Select varieties that are resistant to plant diseases. Some crops for which disease-resistant varieties are available are the following: beans—varieties which resist rust, mildew, and mosaic; cabbage—yellows; cucumbers and cantaloupes—mildew; onions—pink root; peas—wilt; Irish potatoes—late blight; spinach—blight; tomatoes—wilt; and watermelons—wilt and anthracnose.

Some varieties are more resistant to cold or heat than others. For example, 'Charleston Wakefield' and 'Drumhead Savoy' cabbage will withstand temperatures 10° to 15° lower than will 'Copenhagen'. This can be very important when setting early.

Tomato varieties such as 'Marion', 'Manalucie', 'Manapal', and 'Atkinson' are good for late plantings in many areas because their foliage is dense enough to protect fruits from sunscald.

Don't plant a garden that is too large to take care of. A small, well-tended garden is far more rewarding and encouraging than a large, poorly kept one.

5

| Nutritional Group | Vegetable ( ) indicates number of plantings for fresh use | Vitamin Content[1] | | Approximate Planting Per Person | |
|---|---|---|---|---|---|
| | | A | C | Fresh | Freezing or Canning |
| GROUP I High in Vitamins A and C | Spinach (2) | 11,790 | 30 | 8– 12 ft. | 10–15 ft. |
| | Turnip Greens (2) | 10,600 | 60 | 5– 10 ft. | 10–15 ft. |
| | Kale | 8,380 | 51 | 5– 10 ft. | 10–15 ft. |
| | Collards | 7,630 | 44 | 6– 10 ft. | 5–10 ft. |
| | Mustard Greens (2) | 7,180 | 45 | 5– 10 ft. | 10–15 ft. |
| | Cantaloupes | 3,420 | 33 | 3– 5 hls. | 3– 5 hls. |
| | Broccoli | 3,400 | 74 | 5– 10 plts. | 5–10 plts. |
| GROUP II High in Vitamin A | Carrots | 12,500 | 5 | 5– 10 ft. | 10–15 ft. |
| | Swiss Chard (2) | 9,690 | 17 | 5– 10 ft. | 10–15 ft. |
| | Sweet Potatoes | 9,510 | 23 | 10– 20 plts. | |
| | Winter Squash | 6,190 | 7 | 3– 5 hls. | |
| GROUP III High in Vitamin C | Tomatoes | 1,100 | 23 | 3– 5 plts. | 5–10 plts. |
| | Peppers | 740 | 99 | 3– 5 plts. | 3– 5 plts. |
| | Cabbage | 90 | 31 | 5– 10 plts. | 5–10 plts. |
| | Chinese Cabbage | 260 | 31 | 5– 10 ft. | |
| | Cauliflower | 90 | 28 | 4– 6 plts. | 10–15 plts. |
| | Kohlrabi | Trace | 37 | 4– 6 ft. | 6–10 ft. |
| GROUP IV Other Green Vegetables | Asparagus | 1,040 | 23 | 10– 15 hls. | 10–15 hls. |
| | Peas (English) | 720 | 15 | 20– 30 ft. | 40–60 ft. |
| | Green Beans | | | | |
| | Bush (3) | 660 | 14 | 10– 15 ft. | 15–20 ft. |
| | Pole (2) | 660 | 14 | 3– 5 hls. | 3– 5 hls. |
| | Okra | 740 | 20 | 3– 5 ft. | 5–10 ft. |
| GROUP V Starchy Vegetables | Potatoes | 20 | 15 | 50–100 ft. | |
| | Onions (Dry) | 50 | 9 | 50– 75 ft. | |
| | Sweet Corn (3) | 390[2] | 8 | 5– 10 ft. | 30–50 ft. |
| | Lima Beans | | | | |
| | Bush (2) | 290 | 15 | 10– 15 ft. | 15–25 ft. |
| | Pole | 290 | 15 | 3– 5 hls. | 3– 5 hls. |
| | Peas (Field) | 370 | 2 | 10– 15 ft. | 15–25 ft. |
| GROUP VI Other Vegetables | Beans (Wax) | 120 | 5 | 10– 15 ft. | 10–20 ft. |
| | Beets | 20 | 7 | 5– 10 ft. | 10–20 ft. |
| | Cucumbers | 0[3] | 8 | 3– 5 hls. | 3– 5 hls. |
| | Eggplants | 30 | 5 | 2– 3 plts. | 2– 3 plts. |
| | Lettuce (Head) | 540 | 8 | 8– 12 ft. | |
| | Lettuce (Leaf) (3) | 1,620 | 18 | 3– 5 ft. | |
| | Onions (Green) | 50 | 24 | 10– 15 ft. | |
| | Pumpkins | 3,400 | — | 3– 5 hls. | |
| | Radishes (3) | 30 | 24 | 3– 5 ft. | |
| | Squash (Summer) | 260 | 11 | 2– 3 hls. | |
| | Turnips | Trace | 18 | 5– 10 ft. | 5–10 ft. |
| | Watermelons | 590 | 6 | 3– 5 hls. | |

1. Figures for vitamin content were taken from USDA Handbook 8, "Composition of Foods."

Figures indicate amounts per 100-gram sample for cooked vegetables (unless vegetable is normally eaten raw). Vitamin A is expressed in International Units (I.U.); vitamin C, in milligrams (mg.); 100 grams is about 1/2 cup.

The average active adult requires about 5,000 I.U. of vitamin A and 75 mg. of vitamin C in his daily diet.

Vitamin C values are higher if the vegetable is eaten raw—example: cauliflower, 28 mg., cooked,; 69 mg., raw.

2. Only yellow corn contains vitamin A.
3. Pared cucumbers contain no vitamin A.

Even a very small vegetable garden can provide both hours of enjoyment and good eating. Salad greens, snap beans, tomatoes, peppers, and many others require only a minimum of space.

Consider table quality. Sometimes new varieties are bred for disease resistance and shipping qualities, but they may not be as tender as other varieties. On the other hand some varieties are developed for commercial canning or freezing and are superior to standby varieties in these qualities.

Several vegetable diseases can be transmitted on or in the seed. When buying seed deal with a seedman whose integrity you have come to trust or one who is respected by your neighbors. Many dealers offer seed already treated for seed-borne diseases. Many seed are produced in the arid West where humid weather diseases are not a problem and are less likely to carry diseases than are locally grown seed. This is especially true of bean seed. Buy certified seed as noted on the seed packet; this gives you more assurance that the seed will grow true to variety and be free of disease and weed seed.

If you have trouble locating and buying plants of the variety you want consider growing your own plants for transplanting.

Varieties that mature early are important in the arid sections of the country.

### STAGGERED PLANTINGS

By making new plantings of each vegetable at 2- to 4-week intervals, you can be assured of a continuous supply of fresh vegetables throughout the growing season. In snow-free regions of the country, staggered plantings may be a desirable alternative to canning and freezing. Grow corn, beans, tomatoes, and other warm-weather crops in the summer garden, and grow cabbage, turnips, and lettuce in the fall, winter, and early spring gardens. Regionalized planting schedules appear on the seed packets.

Rotate crops (plant them in different places) when growing successive crops in a single growing season.

Take into account the anticipated frost dates in your area. (Refer to Map 1 and Map 2 in

**RADISH**
→ LONG WHITE ICICLE

The variety name appears on the seed package.

Homegrown vegetables make any meal tastier, less expensive, and more satisfying.

Chapter Two, "Planting the Garden.") Plant frost-tender crops only during the frost-free months of the year. Cool-weather crops grow best in the spring and fall.

TOOLS AND EQUIPMENT

A few basic hand tools will be necessary for growing a vegetable garden. A hoe, garden rake, spade, and trowel are indispensable. A powered tiller will be required to turn the soil unless your garden is quite small; then a spade will do the job. Tillers are available in a wide variety of models and prices or for rent. In dry regions, irrigation may be necessary.

Other materials that will prove helpful include polyethylene plastic (black and clear), a supply of hay, pine straw, shredded bark, stakes, fertilizer, and sprayers for applying pesticides.

INSECTS AND DISEASES

Insect and disease management in the home garden is not nearly as difficult as in times past. Judicious use of pesticides can bring about a favorable balance of beneficial and destructive elements and plenty of tasty, nutritious vegetables.

A relatively small number of the thousands of known insects are serious pests of vegetable plants. Many can be controlled simply by picking them off. Others will have to be sprayed or dusted with insecticide (bug killer). Spraying is more effective than dusting, so include a small hand sprayer on your shopping list. The types of insecticides available and methods of using them are treated in Chapter Five, "Controlling Garden Pests."

Virus, fungus, and bacterial diseases may make an appearance during the gardening season, especially during warm, wet years. Check with the County Agricultural Agent to find out which diseases to expect and what resistant varieties of vegetables are available. Should you need to apply a fungicide, the insecticide sprayer can be used. Rinse it out after each use.

## Arranging Crops in the Garden

If some thought is given to arranging crops in the garden, the job of cultivating and replanting sections (after early crops are through bearing) will be easier. No standard plan is best for all gardens, but generally, if your garden is sloping, run your rows on the contour; if it is level, run the rows north and south. By following this practice, low-growing crops will not be shaded as much by the taller ones.

Vegetables should be grouped in the garden. The following blocks suggest groupings that

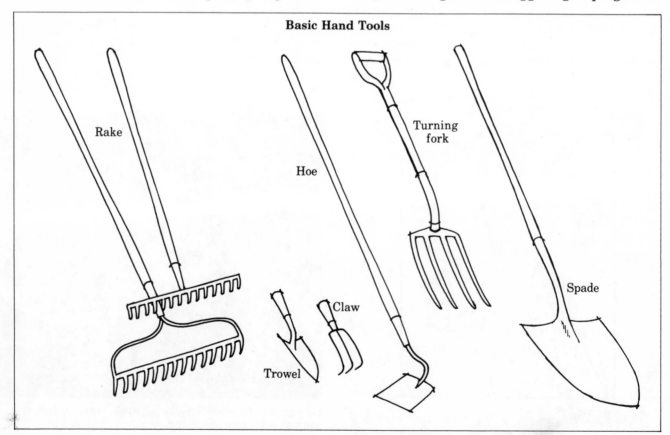

**Basic Hand Tools**

Rake

Hoe

Turning fork

Spade

Claw

Trowel

work well together. Note that not everyone will have room for all the vegetables mentioned, nor will everyone like all of them. Choose those within each group that best suit your taste, and plant them in blocks together.

*Block I.* On one side of the garden, plant perennial crops (those which occupy the same ground for more than 2 years). These perennial crops include asparagus, artichokes, herbs, and strawberries. If one side of the garden is higher than the other, plant these crops on the higher side to lessen late-frost damage and to allow better air circulation in the rest of the garden.

*Block II.* Starting on either side of the garden plant the frost-hardy (or cool-season) crops. Within this block group together the quick-maturing crops: radishes, turnip greens, mustard greens, leaf or Bibb lettuce, spinach, and green onions. Then work your way across this section with those crops that mature in progressively longer periods: English peas, beets, carrots, Swiss chard, kale, head lettuce, collards, kohlrabi, broccoli, cabbage, cauliflower, onions for bulbs, and early Irish potatoes. These vegetables do not have to be planted at the same time.

If your rows are long, several different crops that mature at about the same time may be planted in the same row. Sections of this block will be available in time for planting summer vegetables. It is easier to prepare several rows at one time for replanting than it is to prepare one row or a part of one.

*Block III.* The frost-tender (or warm-season) vegetables can also be grouped according to maturity dates. You may like to consider three subgroups within this block: 1) Bush-type plants (in order of maturity)—summer squash, snap beans, lima beans, Southern peas (such as black-eyed, purple hull, and crowder types), peppers, and tomatoes; 2) Vining plants—cucumbers, cantaloupes, winter squash, watermelons, pumpkins, and sweet potatoes; 3) Tall-growing plants—sweet corn, pole beans, and staked tomatoes. Some people like to plant pole beans next to a fence which can serve as a trellis. In planting corn remember that at least three or four short rows will insure better pollination than two long rows.

*Rotation.* Do not plant the same vegetable in the same part of the garden each year. Let 2 or 3 years pass before replanting a vegetable in the same place. Rotation of vegetables will help keep soil diseases and nematodes from building up. Make a plan or rough sketch of where crops are planted each year to help you rotate crops

properly. To rotate crops, simply start on a different side of the garden each year or rearrange them within each "block."

SELECTING A SITE

Locate the vegetable garden in full sunlight or where it will receive at least 6 hours of direct sunlight every day. A few vegetables (squash, lettuce, pumpkins, melons) will tolerate partial shade, especially in the South, but most require full sun for best production. Avoid locating near large trees; they cast a dense shade and their roots compete with the garden plants for moisture and nutrients in the soil. Some trees, such as black walnuts, exude substances from their roots that may be toxic to other plants.

Locate the vegetable garden as close as possible to your house. Aside from its convenience, the garden's proximity to the house may discourage pests, such as rabbits and woodchucks.

Don't plant too near trees and shrubs; they cast shade and compete with the garden plants near them for moisture and soil nutrients. Note how growth improves farther away from tree.

**Soil**

Garden soil must be well drained; that is, rainwater must pass through it easily without collecting and keeping the roots of the plants waterlogged. Seed planted in soggy soil usually rot. If they do germinate (sprout), the plants will be sickly—if they live at all.

Locate on a slope, or grade the garden plot to slope gently. This will assure that excess water, which the garden soil can't readily absorb, will drain away.

The soil itself should be loose and crumbly. Roots, especially those of tiny seedling plants, cannot penetrate tight, dry soil. Excessively sandy soil, on the other hand, permits water to drain too rapidly, before the plants can benefit from it, and may not anchor plants sufficiently. Deep, sandy loam with a clay subsoil is the ideal soil for vegetable gardening.

Drainage tiles can be the solution for soggy, poorly drained garden plots. Dig a trench 1 to 2 feet deep that slopes to take *advantage of gravity.* Begin the line in the center of the problem area, and run the line to a place where it can drain harmlessly. Lay the tiles in the trench, and wrap each joint (where two tiles meet) with polyethylene plastic or tar paper.

Place terminal tiles at angles to the main drainage line to further disperse the flow of excess moisture.

Pile stones or large pieces of broken crockery around the mouth of the drainage line to prevent clogging. You may wish to fill in around the tiles with gravel before recovering the trench with soil.

Garden soil can be improved by adding organic matter such as grass clippings, hay, pine straw, rotted sawdust, rotted leaves, or peat moss to the soil before planting. Organic matter makes clay soil looser and more porous and makes sandy soil firmer, more moisture-retentive. Clay soils also benefit from the addition of sand, if it is readily available.

If you are preparing soil in the fall for use the following spring, you can condition your soil the way many farmers do by growing a "green manure" cover crop. This consists of planting the garden area with a crop whose sole purpose is to be tilled into the soil after it matures. The cover crop then decomposes in the garden soil, improving soil structure and texture and adding small quantities of nutrient to the soil as decomposition becomes advanced. Crops often grown for this purpose (and easily available to the gardener) include rye, buckwheat, alfalfa, flax, and soybeans. See Chapter Ten, "Organic Vegetable Gardening," for a list of cover crops.

## Soil Test

Vegetables will not grow well in soil that is extremely acid (sour) or alkaline (sweet). A soil test is the most precise method of determining the soil acidity as well as the exact fertilizing requirements of your garden soil. A pH of 7.0 is neutral. Below 7.0, the soil is acid; above 7.0, it is alkaline. Good garden soil has a pH of 5.5 to 7.0. In humid areas, the soil is generally somewhat acid and becomes more acid under cultivation. Adding lime corrects excessive acidity and helps the soil to release phosphorus, potash, and calcium—all vital elements—to the plants. Excessively alkaline soils may be corrected with the addition of ammonium sulfate or other acid-forming materials.

The office of your County Extension Agent will tell you how to collect soil samples to be analyzed. The telephone directory lists the county agent's office under the county government.

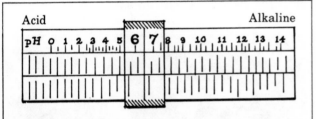

The standard of measurement for soil acidity is pH. A pH of about 7.0 is neutral; below 7.0 the soil is acid and above 7.0 the soil is alkaline.

Collect a pint of soil to send to the soil testing laboratory of your state's soil conservation department. Your County Agricultural Agent (listed in the telephone directory under county government) will send you the proper container and address to which you should send the soil sample.

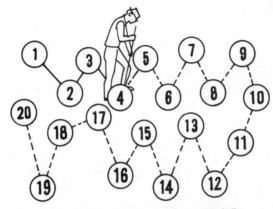

Take 1 teaspoon of soil from about 20 different spots in the garden area. Mix these together thoroughly in the soil sample container.

## A Sample Soil Test Report

Note the precise detail of the recommendations for fertilizer that a soil analysis provides.

REPORT ON SOIL TESTS
AUBURN UNIVERSITY
SOIL TESTING LABORATORY
AUBURN, ALABAMA 36830

PAGE

NAME Martha Fazie
ADDRESS 1149 Loosestrife Ln.
CITY Weigela, Alabama

COUNTY Jefferson
DISTRICT 4
DATE 06/17/75

| LAB NO. | SENDER'S SAMPLE DESIGNATION | SOIL GROUP | SOIL TEST RESULTS | | | | | CROP TO BE GROWN | RECOMMENDATIONS | | | | |
|---|---|---|---|---|---|---|---|---|---|---|---|---|---|
| | | | pH** | PHOSPHORUS P*** | POTASSIUM K*** | MAGNESIUM Mg*** | CALCIUM Ca*** | | LIME-STONE TONS/ACRE | TO SUPPLY Mg | N | P₂O₅ POUNDS PER ACRE | K₂O |
| 47178 1 | 1 | 2 | 6.1 | VH 320 | H 160 | H 640 | **** | GARDEN | 0.0 | | 120 | 0 | 0 |
| | ***COMMENT 73.*** PER 100 FT. OF ROW, APPLY 0.4 LB. N (1 PINT AMMONIUM NITRATE OR EQUIVALENT) AT PLANTING. SIDEDRESS WITH 0.4 LB. N. | | | | | | | | | | | | |
| 47179 1 | 2 | 2 | 6.7 | EH 740 | M 80 | H 340 | **** | AZALEAS | 0.0 | | 120 | 0 | 60 |
| | ***COMMENT 111.*** PHOSPHORUS IS EXCESSIVE AND FERTILIZERS CONTAINING THIS ELEMENT SHOULD NOT BE USED. EXCESSIVE PHOSPHORUS MAY CAUSE AN IRON DEFICIENCY. THE SYMPSOMS OCCUR AS A GENERAL YELLOWING OF NEW GROWTH. TO CORRECT, SPRAY WITH A SOLUBLE SOURCE OF IRON WHICH CAN BE FOUND AT GARDEN SUPPLY STORES. USE AS DIRECTED | | | | | | | | | | | | |
| | ***COMMENT 93.*** PER 100 SQ. FT. APPLY 1 PINT 15-0-15 IN EARLY SPRING AND THEN APPLY 1 CUP AMMONIUM NITRATE OR EQUIVALENT IN EARLY SUMMER. | | | | | | | | | | | | |
| | THE NUMBER OF SAMPLES PROCESSED IN THIS REPORT IS 2. SOLUBLE IRON SOLUTION MUST BE SPRAYED ON LEAVES EVERY 2 WEEKS SINCE PLANTS CANNOT GET THE IRON THEY NEED FROM THE SOIL. | | | | | | | | | | | | |

* 1. Sandy soils
2. Loams & light clays
3. Heavy clays of the Blackbelt

4. Sandy loams of North Alabama
5. Heavy red clays of the limestone valleys

** 7.4 or higher   Alkaline
6.6-7.3   Neutral
6.5 or lower   Acid
5.5 or lower   Very acid

*** Rating & fertility index (percent sufficiency)

APPROVED

SOIL TESTING FORM B

PREPARING THE SOIL FOR PLANTING

In most areas of the country spring is a rainy season. Don't attempt to turn the soil when it is too wet. If the soil sticks in a ball when you squeeze a handful, it is too wet. Small gardens can be covered with polyethylene plastic (black or clear) for a week or two prior to planting to allow the soil to dry out. For this to be effective, however, the garden must have enough of a slope to allow rainwater to run off and not collect in a pool on the plastic. When the soil crumbles as you attempt to squeeze it into a ball, it is ready to be turned.

The best tool for turning the soil is a rotary tiller. Tillers are readily available through garden supply centers and rental agencies. Tilling services are often advertised in the classified pages of the local newspaper. Turn the soil thoroughly, grinding the turf and clods of soil to a fine, crumbly texture. For best results, till to a depth of 6 to 10 inches.

Distribute grass clippings, rotted leaves, hay, and other organic matter over the tilled surface; then sprinkle fertilizer and lime on the organic matter according to the recommendations of a soil test. If you do not have the soil tested, a safe recommendation for fertilizer is about 20 pounds of fertilizer per 1,000 square feet of garden area. To determine the area in square feet, multiply the length of the garden by its width. A 35- × 30-foot plot, for example, is 1,050 square feet. Use a complete fertilizer such as 8-8-8, 10-6-4, or manure. The three numbers found on the fertilizer label indicate the relative percentages *by weight* of the three primary fertilizing elements, nitrogen, phosphorus, and potassium. An analysis of 8-8-8, for instance, indicates that the fertilizer contains 8% nitrogen, 8% phosphoric acid, and 8% potassium oxide.

Till fertilizer and organic matter into the soil until the soil has a uniform, crumbly, slightly spongy texture.

Delay planting at least 2 weeks after this initial soil preparation to allow time for the fertilizer to react with the soil.

A rotary tiller is the best tool for preparing garden soil. The rotating tynes (blades) under the rounded hood on the back of the machine turn up the soil and grind it to a fine, loose texture.

Small areas can be prepared by hand. Turn the soil with a spade or turning fork, and break up clods.

Till the soil until it is loose and crumbly. Remove sticks, stones, and large clods of clay with a garden rake.

Spread grass clippings, rotted leaves, compost (shown here), or other organic matter over the soil, and turn it under with a rotary tiller or a spade. Organic matter improves soil texture and fertility.

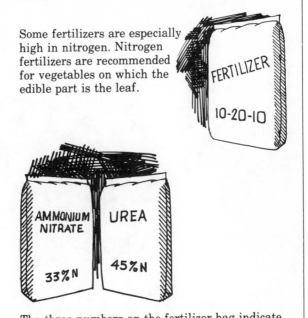

Some fertilizers are especially high in nitrogen. Nitrogen fertilizers are recommended for vegetables on which the edible part is the leaf.

FERTILIZER 10-20-10

AMMONIUM NITRATE 33%N

UREA 45%N

The three numbers on the fertilizer bag indicate the amounts of nitrogen, phosphorus, and potassium in the fertilizer: in this case 10% N (nitrogen), 20% P (phosphorus), and 10% K (potassium).

LIMING GARDEN SOIL

If your soil test indicates a need for lime, use dolomitic lime (builder's lime), available at a nursery or garden supply store, and follow application instructions carefully. Too much lime can damage some crops. Do not apply lime if you do not have the soil tested. Broadcast lime with fertilizer over the garden area before the ground is broken. Using a tiller or disc harrow, work the fertilizer and lime into the soil at least 1 week before planting to allow time for the lime to react properly with the soil.

## Composting

Composting is a practical way of improving your garden soil and disposing of yard refuse at the same time. Compost is decomposed organic matter such as grass clippings, leaves, vegetable garbage from the kitchen, and weeds. Decomposition of this material produces *humus* which, added to the garden, improves moisture retention, soil structure, and fertility. A garden that receives regular applications of compost needs little, if any, additional fertilizer.

The process of decomposition of organic matter is greatly accelerated if the material is gathered into a pile (called a compost heap), kept moist, and turned occasionally. It is well worth the trouble of building a small bin for the compost heap.

A shredder is a great asset to the home gardener. Note how the pile of plant refuse on the right is being chopped into the fine matter you see inside the bin. This ground plant material can be used as mulch, or it can be composted.

MAKING COMPOST

Here are two methods of making compost. The first uses fine, readily decomposable materials and provides compost in about 3 weeks. The second uses coarser materials as well as readily decomposable matter and provides compost in 3 months.

QUICK COMPOST

Follow these steps to construct a cage and to make compost in 3 weeks:

1. Cut a 3-foot wide section of turkey wire or similar wire mesh to a length of 9 or 10 feet. Join the ends to form a circular cage.
2. In this cage collect leaves, hay, weeds, grass clippings, garden refuse (except for coarse materials, such as cornstalks), sawdust or any other plant matter that will break down fairly rapidly. Make a pile about 2 inches thick.
3. Over this sprinkle handfuls of cottonseed meal, alfalfa meal, soybean meal, bone meal, or any other high-protein meal or extract. It is most important to use a meal, because chemical fertilizer will not work. Make sure the organic

matter in the bottom of the cage is thoroughly covered.

4. Repeat steps 2 and 3. Moisten the pile after adding each layer, but do not soak it. Pull the material from the center to the sides, leaving a slight depression in the center. Press the material around the edge to compact it, but leave the center of the pile loose and concave. Be sure each layer is covered with meal.
5. Repeat steps 2 through 4 until the cage is full or until the material is used up. Add more layers as organic material becomes available. Moisten the entire pile.
6. The temperature in the center of the pile should reach 140° to 150° F. within 3 days. Turn the pile after 1 week. Lift the cage off the pile, and refill it, moving the drier material from the edge of the pile into the center of the new pile. Moisten the pile again as you fork it back into the cage. The heating process will start up again. The compost is ready to use when its temperature drops—in 3 weeks. Place your hand against a shaded side of the pile to determine the heat level.

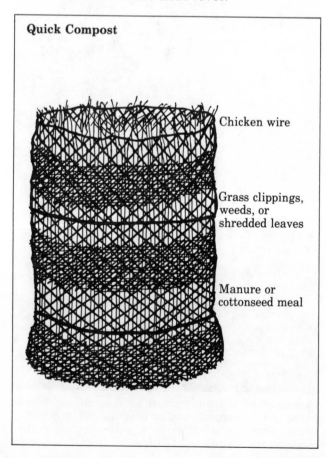

**Quick Compost**

Chicken wire

Grass clippings, weeds, or shredded leaves

Manure or cottonseed meal

## CONVENTIONAL COMPOST

You may use any organic matter that would be suitable for the quick compost, plus coarser materials such as cornstalks and other garden refuse. A sturdier cage is also helpful as the materials will be composting longer; it will also keep the heap from spreading out and becoming unsightly. To compost coarser materials follow these steps:

1. Make a layer 6 to 8 inches deep, 3 feet long, and 3 feet wide of leaves, hay, pine straw, refuse plants from the garden, and any other organic matter you may have available. Vegetable waste from the kitchen may also be composted.
2. Spread a cupful of lime and a cupful of complete fertilizer (such as 5-10-10, 6-12-6, or 8-8-8) over the layer of organic matter.
3. Cover the layer with 1 or 2 inches of dirt. You also may add manure.
4. Dampen this material with a hose. Do not soak it.
5. Repeat steps 1 through 4, building the compost pile in layers.
6. Moisten the finished heap. Again, do not soak it. Commercial materials which

"seed" the pile with bacteria are also available.

Keep the compost pile covered with a black plastic tarp to prevent drying. The cover will also retard the loss of fertilizer in the pile through evaporation and leaching (draining).

Water the heap every other day for 2 weeks. In the sixth week fork the entire heap over into a new pile, and allow it to remain until it is well rotted. After it is thoroughly decomposed (3 to 6 months), it is ready to use.

The best approach to making compost is to start two piles using both methods. This procedure will supply some compost for almost immediate use and will also allow the disposal of coarser materials, which will be ready to use in 3 to 6 months.

Growing tansy and rue around the compost heap will help control flies. The odor, caused by the fermentation process in the pile, will not be objectionable if the compost heap is well tended and turned frequently. When turning the compost shake the clumps of material loose, and then fork it back into the compost bin. Keep the center of the pile loose. The process of decomposition depends on effective penetration of water and air into the pile.

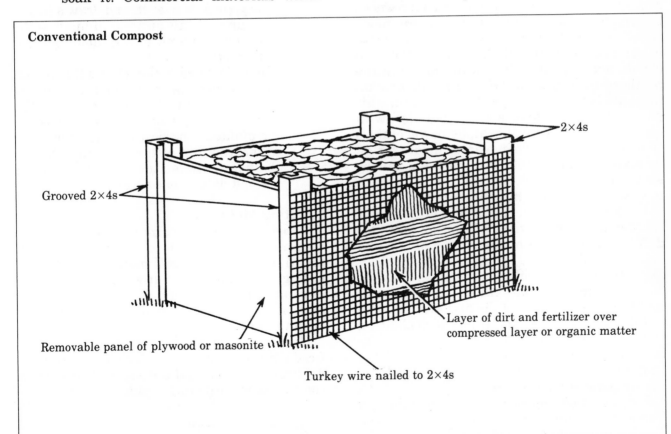

**Conventional Compost**

2×4s

Grooved 2×4s

Removable panel of plywood or masonite

Turkey wire nailed to 2×4s

Layer of dirt and fertilizer over compressed layer or organic matter

# Planting the Garden

## When to Plant

One of the most important elements of success in growing vegetables is planting or transplanting each crop at the time or times that are best for the operation in each locality. Temperatures often differ so much between localities not many miles apart that the best planting dates for a vegetable may differ by several days or even 2 weeks.

Vegetable crops may be roughly grouped and sown according to their hardiness and their temperature requirements. The frost-free date in spring is usually 2 to 3 weeks later than the average date of the last freeze in a locality and is approximately the date that oak trees leaf out.

The gardener should make the first planting of each vegetable as early as he can without too much danger of its being damaged by cold. Many vegetables are so hardy to cold that they can be planted a month or more before the average date of the last freeze, or about 6 weeks before the frost-free date. Furthermore, most, if not all, cold-tolerant crops actually thrive better in cool weather than in hot weather and should not be planted late in the spring in the southern two-thirds of the country where summers are hot. Thus, the gardener must time his planting not only to escape cold but also, with certain crops, to escape heat. Some vegetables that will not thrive when planted in late spring in areas having rather hot summers can be sown in late summer, so that they will make most of their growth in cooler weather.

A gardener anywhere in the United States can determine his own safe planting dates for different crops by using Map 1 and Map 2 and Table 1 and Table 2, published by the U.S. Department of Agriculture. The maps show the average dates of the last killing frosts in spring and the average dates of the first killing frosts in fall. These are the dates from which planting times can be determined, and these determinations have been worked out in Tables 1 and 2 so that any gardener can use them to find the planting dates for his locality.

For example, opposite each vegetable in Table 1, the first date in any column is the *earliest generally safe* date that the crop can be sown or transplanted by the gardener using that column. (No gardener needs to use more than one of the columns.) The second date is the latest date that is likely to prove satisfactory for the planting. All times in between these two dates may not, however, give equally good results. Most of the crops listed do better when planted on, or soon after, the earlier date shown.

To determine the best time to plant any vegetable in the spring in your locality:

1. Find your location on Map 1, then locate the solid line on the map that comes nearest to it.
2. Find the date shown on the solid line. This is the average date of the last killing frost. The first number represents the month; the second number, the day. Thus, 3-10 is March 10. Once you know the date, you are through with the map.
3. Turn to Table 1; find the column that has your date over it; and draw a heavy line around this entire column. It is the only date column in the table that you will need.
4. Find the dates in the column that are on a line with the name of the crop you want to plant. These dates show the period during which the crop can safely be planted. The best time is on, or soon after, the first of the two dates. A time halfway between them is very good; the second date is not as good.

## Planting Methods

Depending upon the size and layout of your garden, you will want to use the method of planting that lends itself most readily to irrigating, fertilizing, and cultivating. The amount of rainfall in your area will be another consideration as will the particular vegetables you wish to grow.

Here are a few of the most commonly practiced methods of planting. Each lends itself to a particular purpose and is designed to help overcome specific gardening problems.

### SIMPLE ROW PLANTING

This basic planting method will suffice for most gardens. Simply make small furrows (trenches) with a hoe, sow seed at the proper intervals, then cover the planted furrow with the displaced soil. Firm the soil over the planted row. Most seed packets indicate the correct depth at which to sow, the correct intervals between seed, and the minimum space between rows.

Most seed packages recommend sowing seed heavily, then thinning out the seedling plants. Another approach is to sow the seed at longer intervals to avoid thinning and to economize on seed.

For planting large seed in a flat row, use the head of the hoe to make a shallow furrow.

Cover the seed with soil, leaf mold, or compost.

For small seed, make a shallow furrow with the handle of a hoe or rake.

Firm soil over the planted seed row.

## RAISED ROWS

In areas where rainfall is heavy excess moisture may collect on the soil surface, causing seed and plant roots to rot. In addition torrential rainfall may wash soil away. These problems can be eliminated, or at least minimized, by mounding the soil into a row and planting the seed along the top. Moisture drains more rapidly from the raised row. Raised rows can also better resist erosion. If you are planting on a slope make the raised rows across the slope rather than up and down the slope. Raised rows will need to be watered during dry spells.

## HILL PLANTING

Hill planting is a popular method of growing pumpkins, squash, melons, cucumbers, and other vine crops. Mound soil about 8 inches high, and press 8 to 10 seeds into the mound in a circle near the top. As plants reach 5 or 6 inches, leave the healthiest 4 or 5 plants, and trim out the rest. Train the plants that are left to radicate out from the mound. Depending on the plant, space mound 3 to 5 feet apart in all directions.

## BED PLANTING

This method permits the most decorative possibilities for small gardens. Instead of planting in rows, mark off areas within the garden plot that are wider than rows but not so wide that you can't reach the center of the bed

Raised rows allow faster drainage and evaporation than flat rows. Use raised rows in regions of high rainfall or in poorly drained soil.

For a hill planting, mound soil 6 to 8 inches high, then plant 6 to 10 seeds around the top of the mound, and cover them with soil.

Planting small gardens in beds instead of rows is a good practice. The decorative effect is enhanced and, more importantly, the beds can be raised well above the level of surrounding soil if drainage is a problem.

from the edge. Sow seed thickly (to crowd out weeds), and thin out seedlings as they develop. Use only low-growing, compact plants such as lettuce, carrots, beets, cabbage, broccoli, cauliflower, spinach, chard, and plants of similar growth habit for bed plantings. Then edge the beds with low-growing flowers or herbs. Mixed beds are also attractive. Try combinations of beets and spinach, carrots and onions, or cabbage and cauliflower. The beds will be further enhanced if they are edged with stones or wood. Beds may be any shape, with neat paths winding between them.

DEPTH AND SPACING

Most seed packets indicate the correct planting depth and spacing of seed. In general large seed is planted twice as deep as its diameter, and small seed is sown on the surface and covered with about 1/4-inch soil or compost. Seed of any size should be planted a little deeper in sandy soil than in clay soil. Seed planted during summer and fall should be placed deeper than those planted in early spring.

If you plant-cultivate with a tiller or small tractor, leave plenty of space between rows (2 to 3 feet). Mulched gardens or those cultivated by hand need not be as roomy; paths 1 foot wide between rows will suffice. The closer the spacing, the better; as garden plants grow, they will shade out weeds. Do not space plants or rows too close together, however, or your plants may be stunted. Thin seedling plants as necessary to allow room for growth. Use the size of mature plants as a guide to thinning.

## Transplanting

Transplanting, or moving a live plant from one location to another, is often necessary in the vegetable garden. When it becomes necessary to thin seedlings, for example, you can transplant rather than discard them. Among the easiest plants to transplant are beets, broccoli, cabbage, cauliflower, celery, chard, eggplant, kale, lettuce, peppers, and tomatoes.

Some vegetables may be grown from small plants rather than seed. The advantages of this are twofold: first, you have a head start with plants, and, second, you do not have to nurse the seed of difficult plants such as onions or celery.

If you buy plants in flats (shallow boxes) remove them with a large spoon and plant them in the garden. Some plants, such as tomatoes, are sold in pots made of pressed peat moss.

There is no need to remove these plants from the pots; roots can grow right through the sides of the pot, and the peat soon decomposes in the soil.

Always use healthy, stocky plants for transplanting. Cover bare-rooted plants (usually wrapped in damp paper) with a damp rag to keep roots from drying out until they are set out in the garden. Set plants out in the late afternoon so that they avoid the stress of the midday summer sun.

Set plants in well-prepared soil. Most plants should be set a little deeper than they grew in the bed. If plants are in peat pots, be sure to completely cover the rim of the pot with soil; otherwise the pot will act as a sponge and draw moisture from soil around the small plant. Pour water around plants to settle the soil around the roots and eliminate air pockets. Better yet, use a weak fertilizer solution, often called "starter" solution.

## Making and Using Starter Solutions

You can get transplanted plants off to a quicker start by using a starter solution when setting them. (Cabbage, collards, tomatoes, peppers, and sweet potatoes respond well to starter solutions.) This solution is not meant to take the place of the regular application of fertilizer, but only to supplement it for early, rapid growth.

For this specific purpose, several commercial mixtures (which dissolve in water much better than regular fertilizer) are available. Be sure to use one with a high content of phosphate, such as 10-52-17, 10-50-10, 15-52-9, or 10-52-8. This high phosphate content promotes rapid growth of new roots.

To make this starter solution, dissolve 2 or 3 pounds of the high phosphate fertilizer in 50 gallons of water. (On a smaller scale, dissolve 1/4 pound (1/2 cup) of the fertilizer in 5 gallons of water or, 1/4 cup in 2 1/2 gallons.)

Pour 1/2 pint of the solution in the hole as each plant is set, using the solution as you would plain water when transplanting.

Regardless of the planting system you use, water the seed rows after planting is completed. Adjust the hose nozzle for a fine spray so that the soil is not disturbed by the stream of water. This will encourage germination of seed and root establishment of transplants. In the earliest stages of life, the roots of the plants will occupy only the top 2 or 3 inches of the soil. It is crucial to the plant's growth that this top layer of soil not be allowed to become too dry.

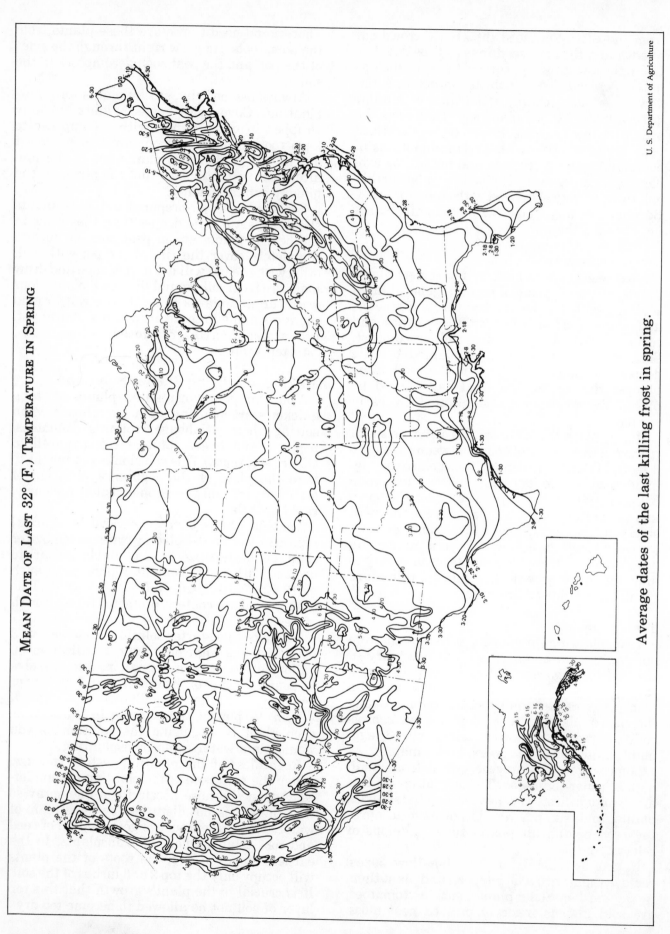

U. S. Department of Agriculture

Average dates of the last killing frost in spring.

## TABLE 1.—Earliest dates, and range of dates, for safe spring planting of vegetables in the open

| Crop | Planting dates for localities in which average date of last freeze is— | | | | | | |
|---|---|---|---|---|---|---|---|
| | Jan. 30 | Feb. 8 | Feb. 18 | Feb. 28 | Mar. 10 | Mar. 20 | Mar. 30 |
| Asparagus¹ | (²) | (²) | (²) | (²) | Jan. 1–Mar. 1 | Feb. 1–Mar. 10 | Feb. 15–Mar. 20 |
| Beans, lima | Feb. 1–Apr. 15 | Feb. 10–May 1 | Mar. 1–May 1 | Mar. 15–June 1 | Mar. 20–June 1 | Apr. 1–June 15 | Apr. 1–June 20 |
| Beans, snap | Feb. 1–Apr. 1 | Feb. 1–May 1 | Mar. 1–May 1 | Mar. 10–May 15 | Mar. 15–May 25 | Mar. 15–May 25 | Mar. 1–June 1 |
| Beet | Jan. 1–Mar. 15 | Jan. 10–Mar. 15 | Jan. 15–Mar. 15 | Jan. 1–Mar. 15 | Feb. 1–June 1 | Feb. 15–June 1 | Mar. 1–June 1 |
| Broccoli, sprouting¹ | Jan. 1–30 | Jan. 1–30 | Jan. 1–Feb. 15 | Jan. 1–Feb. 15 | Jan. 15–Mar. 15 | Feb. 1–Mar. 15 | Mar. 1–20 |
| Brussels sprouts¹ | Jan. 1–30 | Jan. 1–30 | Jan. 1–Feb. 15 | Jan. 1–Feb. 15 | Jan. 15–Mar. 15 | Feb. 1–Mar. 15 | Mar. 1–20 |
| Cabbage¹ | Jan. 1–15 | Jan. 1–Feb. 10 | Jan. 1–Feb. 15 | Jan. 1–Feb. 15 | Jan. 1–Mar. 15 | Feb. 10–Mar. 10 | Feb. 15–Mar. 10 |
| Cabbage, Chinese | (²) | (²) | (²) | (²) | (²) | (²) | (²) |
| Carrot | Jan. 1–Mar. 1 | Jan. 1–Mar. 1 | Jan. 15–Mar. 1 | Jan. 1–Mar. 1 | Feb. 1–Mar. 1 | Feb. 10–Mar. 10 | Mar. 1–Apr. 10 |
| Cauliflower¹ | Jan. 1–Feb. 1 | Jan. 1–Feb. 1 | Jan. 1–Feb. 15 | Jan. 10–Feb. 10 | Jan. 20–Feb. 20 | Feb. 1–Mar. 1 | Feb. 20–Mar. 20 |
| Celery and celeriac | Jan. 1–Feb. 1 | Jan. 10–Feb. 10 | Jan. 20–Feb. 20 | Feb. 1–Mar. 1 | Feb. 20–May 20 | Mar. 1–Apr. 1 | Mar. 15–Apr. 15 |
| Chard | Jan. 1–Apr. 1 | Jan. 10–Apr. 1 | Jan. 20–Apr. 15 | Feb. 1–May 1 | Feb. 15–May 15 | Feb. 20–May 15 | Mar. 1–May 25 |
| Chervil and chives | Jan. 1–Feb. 1 | Jan. 1–Feb. 1 | Jan. 1–Feb. 1 | Jan. 1–Mar. 1 | Jan. 1–Mar. 1 | Feb. 1–Mar. 1 | Feb. 15–Mar. 15 |
| Chicory, witloof | (²) | (²) | (²) | (²) | June 1–July 1 | June 1–July 1 | June 1–July 1 |
| Collards¹ | Jan. 1–Feb. 15 | Jan. 1–Feb. 15 | Jan. 1–Mar. 15 | Jan. 1–Mar. 15 | Jan. 1–June 1 | Jan. 15–May 1 | Mar. 1–June 1 |
| Corn salad | Jan. 1–Feb. 15 | Jan. 1–Feb. 15 | Jan. 1–Feb. 15 | Jan. 1–Mar. 1 | Jan. 1–Mar. 15 | Jan. 15–Mar. 15 | Jan. 15–Mar. 15 |
| Corn, sweet | Feb. 1–Mar. 15 | Feb. 10–Apr. 1 | Feb. 20–Apr. 15 | Mar. 1–Apr. 15 | Mar. 10–Apr. 15 | Mar. 15–May 1 | Mar. 25–May 15 |
| Cress, upland | Jan. 1–Feb. 1 | Jan. 1–Feb. 15 | Jan. 15–Feb. 15 | Feb. 1–Mar. 1 | Feb. 15–Apr. 15 | Mar. 1–Apr. 15 | Mar. 10–May 15 |
| Cucumber | Feb. 15–Mar. 15 | Feb. 10–Apr. 15 | Feb. 20–Apr. 15 | Mar. 1–Apr. 15 | Apr. 1–May 1 | Apr. 1–May 1 | Apr. 10–May 15 |
| Eggplant¹ | Feb. 1–Mar. 1 | Feb. 10–Apr. 15 | Feb. 20–Apr. 15 | Mar. 1–Apr. 15 | Mar. 15–Apr. 15 | Apr. 1–May 1 | Apr. 15–May 15 |
| Endive | Jan. 1–Mar. 1 | Jan. 1–Mar. 1 | Jan. 1–Mar. 1 | Jan. 1–Mar. 1 | Feb. 15–Mar. 15 | Feb. 1–Apr. 1 | Mar. 15–Apr. 15 |
| Fennel, Florence | Jan. 1–Mar. 1 | Jan. 1–Mar. 1 | Jan. 15–Mar. 1 | Jan. 15–Mar. 1 | Feb. 1–Apr. 1 | Mar. 1–Apr. 1 | Mar. 10–Apr. 10 |
| Garlic | (²) | (²) | (²) | (²) | Feb. 1–Mar. 1 | Feb. 1–Apr. 1 | Mar. 10–Apr. 10 |
| Horseradish¹ | Jan. 1–Feb. 1 | Jan. 1–Feb. 1 | Jan. 1–Feb. 1 | Feb. 1–20 | Feb. 10–Mar. 10 | Feb. 20–Mar. 10 | Mar. 1–Apr. 1 |
| Kale | Jan. 1–Feb. 1 | Jan. 10–Feb. 1 | Jan. 1–Feb. 1 | Feb. 1–20 | Feb. 10–Mar. 10 | Feb. 20–Mar. 10 | Mar. 1–Apr. 1 |
| Kohlrabi | Jan. 1–Feb. 1 | Jan. 10–Feb. 1 | Jan. 1–Feb. 15 | Feb. 1–Mar. 1 | Feb. 10–Mar. 10 | Feb. 20–Mar. 15 | Mar. 1–Apr. 1 |
| Leek¹ | Jan. 1–Feb. 1 | Jan. 1–Feb. 1 | Jan. 1–Feb. 1 | Jan. 1–Mar. 1 | Jan. 1–Mar. 15 | Feb. 1–Apr. 1 | Mar. 15–Apr. 15 |
| Lettuce, head¹ | Feb. 15–Mar. 15 | Feb. 1–Apr. 1 | Jan. 1–Mar. 15 | Jan. 1–Mar. 15 | Jan. 15–Apr. 15 | Feb. 1–Apr. 1 | Mar. 1–20 |
| Lettuce, leaf | Jan. 1–Apr. 1 | Jan. 1–Apr. 1 | Jan. 1–Apr. 15 | Jan. 1–Apr. 15 | Feb. 1–Apr. 15 | Feb. 20–Apr. 1 | Mar. 15–May 15 |
| Muskmelon | Feb. 15–Apr. 1 | Feb. 15–Apr. 15 | Mar. 1–Apr. 15 | Mar. 15–Apr. 15 | Apr. 1–Apr. 15 | Apr. 10–May 15 | Apr. 10–May 15 |
| Mustard | Jan. 1–Mar. 1 | Feb. 1–Mar. 1 | Mar. 1–June 1 | Mar. 10–June 1 | Mar. 20–June 1 | Apr. 1–June 15 | Mar. 1–Apr. 15 |
| Okra | Feb. 15–May 15 | Feb. 1–Feb. 1 | Jan. 1–Feb. 1 | Feb. 1–June 1 | Feb. 15–May 1 | Feb. 15–June 1 | Apr. 10–June 15 |
| Onion¹ | Jan. 1–15 | Jan. 1–15 | Jan. 1–15 | Jan. 1–15 | Jan. 1–Feb. 1 | Feb. 1–Mar. 1 | Feb. 15–Mar. 15 |
| Onion, seed | Jan. 1–15 | Jan. 1–15 | Jan. 1–15 | Jan. 1–15 | Jan. 1–Feb. 1 | Feb. 1–Mar. 1 | Feb. 15–Mar. 15 |
| Onion, sets | Jan. 1–15 | Jan. 1–15 | Jan. 1–15 | Jan. 1–15 | Jan. 15–Mar. 10 | Feb. 1–Mar. 20 | Feb. 20–Mar. 20 |
| Parsley | Jan. 1–30 | Jan. 1–30 | Jan. 1–Mar. 1 | Jan. 1–Mar. 1 | Jan. 15–Mar. 10 | Feb. 1–Mar. 10 | Mar. 1–Apr. 1 |
| Parsnip | Jan. 1–Feb. 15 | Jan. 1–Feb. 15 | Jan. 1–Mar. 1 | Jan. 1–Mar. 1 | Jan. 15–Mar. 15 | Feb. 1–Mar. 15 | Mar. 1–Apr. 1 |
| Peas, garden | Jan. 1–Feb. 15 | Jan. 1–Feb. 15 | Jan. 1–Mar. 1 | Jan. 1–Feb. 15 | Jan. 15–Mar. 15 | Feb. 1–July 1 | Feb. 10–Mar. 20 |
| Peas, black-eyed | Feb. 15–May 1 | Feb. 15–May 1 | Mar. 1–June 15 | Mar. 10–June 20 | Mar. 15–July 1 | Apr. 1–July 1 | Apr. 15–July 1 |
| Pepper¹ | Feb. 1–Apr. 15 | Feb. 15–May 1 | Mar. 1–May 1 | Mar. 15–May 1 | Apr. 1–June 1 | Apr. 10–June 1 | Apr. 15–June 1 |
| Potato | Jan. 1–Feb. 15 | Jan. 1–Feb. 15 | Jan. 15–Mar. 1 | Jan. 15–Mar. 1 | Feb. 1–Mar. 1 | Feb. 10–Mar. 20 | Feb. 20–Mar. 20 |
| Radish | Jan. 1–Apr. 1 | Jan. 1–Apr. 1 | Jan. 1–Apr. 15 | Jan. 1–Apr. 15 | Jan. 1–May 1 | Feb. 1–May 1 | Feb. 15–May 1 |
| Rhubarb¹ | (²) | (²) | (²) | (²) | Jan. 15–Feb. 20 | Feb. 1–Mar. 1 | Feb. 1–Mar. 1 |
| Rutabaga | Jan. 1–Feb. 1 | Jan. 1–Feb. 10 | Jan. 1–Feb. 20 | Jan. 1–Mar. 1 | Jan. 15–Mar. 1 | Feb. 1–Mar. 1 | Mar. 1–15 |
| Salsify | Jan. 1–Feb. 1 | Jan. 1–Feb. 10 | Jan. 1–Mar. 1 | Jan. 1–Mar. 1 | Jan. 15–Mar. 1 | Feb. 1–Mar. 10 | Mar. 15–Apr. 15 |
| Shallot | Jan. 1–Feb. 1 | Jan. 1–Mar. 1 | Jan. 1–Mar. 1 | Jan. 1–Mar. 10 | Feb. 1–Mar. 1 | Feb. 10–Mar. 20 | Feb. 20–Apr. 1 |
| Sorrel | Jan. 1–Mar. 1 | Jan. 1–Mar. 1 | Jan. 15–Mar. 1 | Jan. 20–Mar. 1 | Mar. 1–June 30 | Mar. 10–June 30 | Apr. 20–June 30 |
| Soybean | Mar. 1–June 30 | Mar. 1–June 30 | Mar. 10–June 30 | Mar. 20–June 30 | Apr. 10–June 30 | Apr. 20–June 30 | Feb. 1–Mar. 20 |
| Spinach | Jan. 1–Feb. 15 | Jan. 1–Feb. 10 | Jan. 1–Mar. 1 | Jan. 1–Mar. 1 | Jan. 1–Mar. 1 | Jan. 15–Mar. 15 | Feb. 1–Mar. 20 |
| Spinach, New Zealand | Feb. 1–Apr. 15 | Feb. 15–Apr. 15 | Mar. 1–Apr. 15 | Mar. 1–Mar. 15 | Mar. 15–May 15 | Apr. 1–May 15 | Apr. 10–June 1 |
| Squash, summer | Feb. 1–Apr. 15 | Feb. 15–Apr. 15 | Mar. 1–Apr. 15 | Mar. 15–May 15 | Mar. 20–May 15 | Apr. 1–May 15 | Apr. 10–June 1 |
| Sweet potato | Feb. 15–May 15 | Mar. 1–May 15 | Mar. 20–June 1 | Mar. 20–June 1 | Apr. 1–June 1 | Apr. 10–June 1 | Apr. 20–June 1 |
| Tomato | Feb. 1–Apr. 1 | Feb. 20–Apr. 10 | Mar. 1–Apr. 20 | Mar. 20–Mar. 1 | Mar. 15–May 15 | Apr. 1–May 20 | Apr. 10–June 1 |
| Turnip | Jan. 1–Mar. 1 | Jan. 1–Mar. 1 | Jan. 10–Mar. 1 | Jan. 20–Mar. 1 | Feb. 1–Mar. 1 | Feb. 10–Mar. 10 | Mar. 1–Apr. 15 |
| Watermelon | Feb. 15–Mar. 15 | Feb. 15–Apr. 1 | Mar. 1–Apr. 15 | Mar. 15–Apr. 15 | Apr. 1–May 1 | Apr. 1–May 1 | Apr. 10–May 15 |

¹Plants    ²Generally fall-planted

TABLE 1.—*Earliest dates, and range of dates, for safe spring planting of vegetables in the open—Continued*

| Crop | Planting dates for localities in which average date of last freeze is— | | | | | | |
|---|---|---|---|---|---|---|---|
| | Apr. 10 | Apr. 20 | Apr. 30 | May 10 | May 20 | May 30 | June 10 |
| Asparagus[1] | Mar. 10–Apr. 10 | Mar. 15–Apr. 15 | Mar. 20–Apr. 15 | Mar. 10–Apr. 30 | Apr. 20–May 15 | May 1–June 1 | May 15–June 1. |
| Beans, lima | Apr. 1–June 30 | May 1–June 20 | May 15–June 15 | May 25–June 15 | May 1–June 1 | | |
| Beans, snap | Apr. 10–June 30 | Apr. 25–June 30 | May 10–June 30 | May 10–June 30 | May 15–June 30 | May 25–June 15 | June 15. |
| Beet | Mar. 10–June 1 | Mar. 10–June 1 | Apr. 1–June 15 | Apr. 15–June 15 | Apr. 25–June 15 | May 1–June 15 | May 15–June 15. |
| Broccoli, sprouting[1] | Mar. 15–Apr. 15 | Mar. 25–Apr. 20 | Apr. 1–June 15 | Apr. 15–June 15 | May 1–June 15 | May 1–June 15 | May 10–June 10. |
| Brussels sprouts[1] | Mar. 15–Apr. 15 | Mar. 25–Apr. 20 | Apr. 1–May 1 | Apr. 15–June 1 | May 1–June 15 | May 10–June 10 | May 20–June 10. |
| Cabbage[1] | Mar. 1–Apr. 1 | Mar. 10–Apr. 1 | Mar. 15–Apr. 10 | Apr. 1–May 15 | May 1–June 1 | May 10–June 15 | May 20–June 1. |
| Cabbage, Chinese | (²) | (²) | (²) | (²) | May 1–June 1 | May 10–June 15 | May 20–June 1. |
| Carrot | Mar. 10–Apr. 20 | Apr. 1–May 15 | Apr. 10–June 1 | Apr. 20–June 15 | May 1–June 1 | May 10–June 1 | May 20–June 1. |
| Cauliflower[1] | Mar. 1–Mar. 20 | Mar. 15–Apr. 20 | Apr. 10–May 10 | Apr. 15–May 15 | May 10–June 15 | May 20–June 1 | June 1–June 15. |
| Celery and celeriac | Apr. 1–Apr. 20 | Apr. 10–May 1 | Apr. 15–May 1 | Apr. 20–June 15 | May 10–June 15 | May 20–June 1 | June 1–June 15. |
| Chard | Mar. 15–June 15 | Mar. 15–June 15 | Apr. 1–June 15 | Apr. 15–June 15 | May 1–June 15 | May 20–June 1 | June 1–June 15. |
| Chervil and chives | Mar. 1–Apr. 1 | Mar. 10–Apr. 10 | Apr. 1–May 1 | Apr. 15–May 15 | May 1–May 15 | May 1–June 1 | May 15–June 1. |
| Chicory, witloof | June 10–July 1 | June 15–July 1 | June 15–July 1 | June 1–20 | June 1–15 | June 1–15 | June 1–15. |
| Collards[1] | Mar. 1–June 1 | Mar. 1–June 1 | Mar. 10–June 1 | Apr. 1–June 1 | Apr. 15–June 1 | May 1–June 1 | May 10–June 1. |
| Corn salad | Feb. 1–Apr. 1 | Feb. 15–Apr. 15 | Mar. 1–Apr. 15 | Apr. 1–June 1 | Apr. 15–June 1 | May 1–June 15 | May 15–June 15. |
| Corn, sweet | Apr. 10–June 1 | Apr. 25–June 15 | May 10–June 15 | May 10–June 1 | May 15–June 1 | May 20–June 1 | |
| Cress, upland | Mar. 10–Apr. 15 | Mar. 20–May 1 | Apr. 10–May 10 | Apr. 20–May 20 | May 1–June 1 | May 15–June 1 | May 15–June 15. |
| Cucumber | Apr. 20–June 1 | May 1–June 15 | May 15–June 15 | May 20–June 15 | June 1 | June 15 | |
| Eggplant[1] | May 1–June 1 | May 10–June 1 | May 15–June 10 | May 20–June 15 | June 1–15 | | |
| Endive | Mar. 15–Apr. 15 | Mar. 25–Apr. 15 | Apr. 15–May 15 | May 1–30 | May 15–June 1 | May 15–June 15 | May 15–June 1. |
| Fennel, Florence | Mar. 15–Apr. 15 | Mar. 25–Apr. 15 | Apr. 15–May 15 | May 1–30 | May 15–June 1 | June 1–30 | May 15–June 1. |
| Garlic | Feb. 20–Mar. 20 | Feb. 20–Mar. 20 | Mar. 10–Apr. 1 | Mar. 15–Apr. 15 | Apr. 1–30 | May 1–30 | May 15–June 1. |
| Horseradish[1] | Mar. 10–Apr. 10 | Mar. 20–Apr. 20 | Apr. 1–30 | Apr. 15–May 15 | | | |
| Kale | Mar. 10–Apr. 1 | Mar. 20–Apr. 10 | Apr. 1–20 | Apr. 10–May 1 | Apr. 20–May 10 | May 1–30 | May 15–June 1. |
| Kohlrabi | Mar. 10–Apr. 10 | Mar. 20–May 1 | Apr. 1–May 10 | Apr. 10–May 15 | May 1–30 | May 1–30 | May 15–June 1. |
| Leek | Mar. 1–Apr. 1 | Mar. 1–Apr. 1 | Mar. 15–Apr. 15 | Apr. 1–May 1 | Apr. 1–May 1 | May 1–15 | May 1–15. |
| Lettuce, head[1] | Mar. 10–Apr. 1 | Mar. 20–Apr. 15 | Apr. 1–May 1 | Apr. 15–May 15 | May 1–June 30 | May 10–June 30 | May 20–June 30. |
| Lettuce, leaf | Mar. 15–May 15 | Mar. 20–May 15 | Apr. 1–June 1 | Apr. 15–June 15 | May 1–June 30 | May 10–June 30 | May 20–June 30. |
| Muskmelon | Apr. 20–June 1 | May 1–June 15 | May 15–June 1 | June 15–June 1 | | | |
| Mustard | Mar. 10–Apr. 20 | Mar. 20–May 1 | Apr. 1–May 10 | Apr. 15–June 1 | May 1–June 30 | May 10–June 30 | May 20–June 30. |
| Okra | Apr. 20–June 15 | May 1–June 1 | May 10–June 1 | May 20–June 10 | June 1–20 | June 1–20 | |
| Onion[1] | Mar. 1–Apr. 1 | Mar. 15–Apr. 10 | Apr. 1–May 1 | Apr. 10–May 1 | Apr. 20–May 15 | May 1–30 | May 10–June 10. |
| Onion, seed | Mar. 1–Apr. 1 | Mar. 15–Apr. 1 | Apr. 1–15 | Apr. 10–May 1 | Apr. 20–May 15 | May 1–30 | May 1–June 10. |
| Onion, sets | Mar. 1–Apr. 1 | Mar. 10–Apr. 1 | Apr. 1–15 | Apr. 10–May 1 | Apr. 20–May 15 | May 1–30 | May 1–June 10. |
| Parsley | Mar. 10–Apr. 10 | Mar. 20–May 1 | Apr. 1–May 1 | Apr. 15–May 15 | May 1–20 | May 10–June 1 | May 20–June 10. |
| Parsnip | Mar. 1–Apr. 1 | Mar. 10–Apr. 10 | Apr. 1–May 1 | Apr. 15–May 15 | May 1–20 | May 1–June 1 | May 20–June 10. |
| Peas, garden | Jan. 15–Apr. 1 | Feb. 1–Mar. 15 | Feb. 20–Mar. 20 | Mar. 10–Apr. 1 | Mar. 20–May 1 | Apr. 1–June 15 | May 10–June 15. |
| Peas, black-eyed | May 1–July 1 | May 10–June 15 | May 15–June 15 | May 25–June 10 | June 1 | | |
| Pepper[1] | May 1–June 1 | May 10–June 1 | May 15–June 10 | May 20–June 10 | June 1–15 | | |
| Potato | Mar. 10–Apr. 1 | Mar. 10–Apr. 1 | Mar. 15–June 10 | Apr. 1–June 15 | May 1–June 15 | June 1–15 | May 15–June 1. |
| Radish | Mar. 1–May 1 | Mar. 10–May 10 | Mar. 20–May 10 | Apr. 1–June 1 | Apr. 15–June 15 | May 1–June 15 | May 15–June 15. |
| Rhubarb[1] | Mar. 1–Apr. 1 | Mar. 10–Apr. 10 | Mar. 20–Apr. 15 | Apr. 1–May 1 | Apr. 15–May 10 | May 1–20 | May 20–June 1. |
| Rutabaga | | | | May 1–June 1 | May 1–20 | May 10–20 | |
| Salsify | Mar. 10–Apr. 15 | Mar. 20–May 1 | Apr. 1–June 1 | Apr. 15–June 1 | May 1–June 1 | May 10–20 | May 20–June 1. |
| Shallot | Mar. 1–Apr. 1 | Mar. 15–Apr. 15 | Apr. 1–May 1 | Apr. 10–May 1 | Apr. 20–May 1 | May 1–June 1 | May 1–June 1. |
| Sorrel | Mar. 1–Apr. 15 | Mar. 15–May 15 | Apr. 1–May 15 | Apr. 15–June 1 | May 1–June 1 | May 10–June 10 | May 10–June 1. |
| Soybean | May 1–June 30 | May 1–June 30 | May 15–June 15 | May 25–June 10 | June 1 | | |
| Spinach | Feb. 15–Apr. 1 | Mar. 1–Apr. 15 | Mar. 20–Apr. 20 | Apr. 1–June 15 | Apr. 20–June 15 | May 1–June 15 | May 1–June 15. |
| Spinach, New Zealand | Apr. 20–June 1 | May 1–June 15 | May 1–June 15 | May 10–June 15 | May 20–June 15 | May 20–June 15 | |
| Squash, summer | Apr. 20–June 1 | May 1–30 | May 10–June 10 | May 20–June 15 | June 1–15 | June 1–20 | June 10–20. |
| Sweet potato | May 1–June 1 | May 10–June 10 | May 20–June 10 | June 1 | | | |
| Tomato | Apr. 1–June 1 | Apr. 20–June 10 | May 1–June 15 | May 15–June 10 | May 25–June 15 | June 5–20 | June 15–30. |
| Turnip | Mar. 1–Apr. 1 | Mar. 1–Apr. 1 | Mar. 20–May 1 | Apr. 1–June 1 | Apr. 15–June 1 | May 1–June 15 | May 15–June 15. |
| Watermelon | Apr. 20–June 1 | May 1–June 15 | May 10–June 15 | June 1–June 15 | June 15–July 1 | May 1–June 15 | May 15–June 15. |

[1]Plants    [2]Generally fall-planted

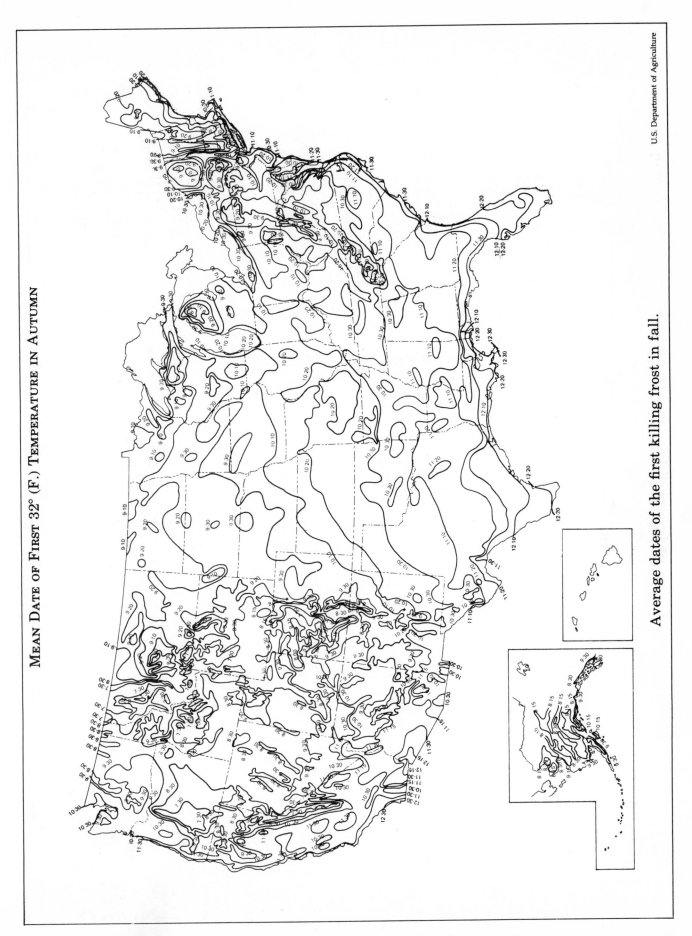

U.S. Department of Agriculture

Average dates of the first killing frost in fall.

## TABLE 2.—*Latest dates, and range of dates, for safe fall planting of vegetables in the open*

| Crop | Planting dates for localities in which average dates of first freeze is— | | | | | |
|---|---|---|---|---|---|---|
| | Aug. 30 | Sept. 10 | Sept. 20 | Sept. 30 | Oct. 10 | Oct. 20 |
| Asparagus¹ | | | | | Oct. 20–Nov. 15 | Nov. 1–Dec. 15. |
| Beans, lima | | | | June 1–15 | June 1–15 | June 15–30. |
| Beans, snap | May 15–June 15 | May 15–June 15 | June 1–July 1 | June 1–July 10 | June 15–July 20 | July 1–Aug. 1. |
| Beet | May 15–June 15 | May 15–June 15 | June 1–July 1 | June 1–July 10 | June 15–July 25 | July 1–Aug. 5. |
| Broccoli, sprouting | May 1–June 1 | May 1–June 1 | May 1–June 15 | June 1–30 | June 15–July 15 | July 1–Aug. 1. |
| Brussels sprouts | May 1–June 1 | May 1–June 1 | May 1–June 15 | June 1–30 | June 15–July 15 | July 1–Aug. 1. |
| Cabbage¹ | May 1–June 1 | May 1–June 1 | May 1–July 1 | June 1–July 10 | June 1–July 15 | July 1–20. |
| Cabbage, Chinese | May 15–June 15 | May 15–June 15 | May 15–July 1 | June 1–July 15 | June 15–Aug. 1 | July 15–Aug. 15. |
| Carrot | May 15–June 15 | May 15–June 15 | May 15–July 1 | June 1–July 10 | June 1–July 20 | July 15–Aug. 15. |
| Cauliflower¹ | May 1–June 1 | May 1–July 1 | May 1–July 1 | June 1–July 1 | June 1–July 25 | July 1–Aug. 5. |
| Celery¹ and celeriac | May 1–June 1 | May 1–June 1 | May 1–June 15 | May 10–July 1 | June 1–July 15 | June 1–Aug. 1. |
| Chard | May 15–June 15 | May 15–July 1 | May 15–July 1 | June 1–July 5 | June 1–July 20 | June 1–Aug. 1. |
| Chervil and chives | May 10–June 10 | May 15–June 15 | May 15–June 15 | June 1–July 5 | | June 1–Aug. 1. |
| Chicory, witloof | May 15–June 15 | May 15–June 15 | May 15–June 15 | June 1–July 1 | (²) | (²) |
| Collards¹ | May 15–June 15 | May 15–July 1 | May 15–June 15 | June 1–July 1 | June 1–July 1 | June 15–July 15. |
| Corn salad | May 15–June 15 | May 15–June 15 | May 15–Aug. 1 | June 15–July 15 | July 1–Aug. 1 | July 15–Aug. 15. |
| Corn, sweet | | | June 1–July 1 | July 15–Sept. 1 | Aug. 15–Sept. 15 | Sept. 1–Oct. 15. |
| Cress, upland | May 15–June 15 | May 15–July 1 | June 15–Aug. 1 | June 1–July 1 | June 1–July 10 | June 1–July 20. |
| Cucumber | | | June 1–15 | July 15–Sept. 1 | Aug. 15–Sept. 15 | Sept. 1–Oct. 15. |
| Eggplant¹ | | | | | June 1–July 1 | June 1–July 15. |
| Endive | June 1–July 1 | June 1–July 1 | June 15–July 15 | June 1–July 15 | July 1–Aug. 15 | July 15–Sept. 1. |
| Fennel, Florence | May 15–June 15 | May 15–July 15 | June 1–July 1 | June 15–Aug. 1 | July 1–Aug. 15 | June 1–Aug. 1. |
| Garlic | (²) | (²) | (²) | June 1–July 1 | June 15–July 15 | June 1–Aug. 1. |
| Horseradish¹ | (²) | (²) | (²) | (²) | (²) | (²) |
| Kale | May 15–June 15 | May 15–June 15 | June 1–July 1 | June 15–July 15 | July 1–Aug. 1 | July 15–Aug. 15. |
| Kohlrabi | May 15–June 15 | June 1–July 1 | June 1–July 15 | June 15–July 15 | July 1–Aug. 1 | July 15–Aug. 15. |
| Leek | May 1–June 1 | May 1–June 1 | May 1–June 1 | | (²) | |
| Lettuce, head¹ | May 15–July 1 | May 15–July 1 | June 1–July 15 | July 1–Aug. 1 | July 15–Aug. 15 | Aug. 1–30. |
| Lettuce, leaf | May 15–July 15 | May 15–July 15 | June 1–Aug. 1 | July 15–Aug. 1 | July 15–Sept. 1 | July 15–Sept. 1. |
| Muskmelon | | | May 15–June 15 | June 15–July 1 | July 15–Aug. 15 | June 15–July 20. |
| Mustard | May 15–July 15 | May 15–July 15 | June 1–Aug. 1 | June 1–Aug. 1 | July 15–Aug. 15 | Aug. 1–Sept. 1. |
| Okra | | | June 1–20 | June 1–July 1 | June 1–Aug. 15 | June 1–July 1. |
| Onion¹ | May 1–June 10 | May 1–June 10 | (²) | (²) | (²) | (²) |
| Onion, seed | May 1–June 1 | May 1–June 10 | (²) | (²) | (²) | (²) |
| Onion, sets | May 1–June 1 | May 1–June 15 | (²) | (²) | (²) | (²) |
| Parsley | May 15–June 15 | May 15–June 15 | June 1–July 1 | June 1–July 15 | July 15–Aug. 15 | July 15–Aug. 15. |
| Parsnip | May 15–June 15 | May 15–June 15 | May 15–June 15 | June 1–July 1 | | |
| Peas, garden | May 10–June 15 | May 1–July 1 | May 1–July 15 | June 1–July 15 | June 15–Aug. 10 | June 1–July 1. |
| Peas, black-eyed | | | | June 1–Aug. 1 | June 1–July 10 | June 1–July 10. |
| Pepper¹ | | | June 1–June 20 | June 1–July 1 | June 1–July 1 | |
| Potato | May 15–June 1 | May 1–June 15 | May 1–June 15 | June 1–July 1 | July 1–Aug. 1 | June 15–July 15. |
| Radish | May 1–July 15 | May 1–Aug. 1 | May 1–Aug. 15 | Sept. 1–Nov. 1 | Sept. 15–Nov. 15 | Aug. 15–Oct. 1. |
| Rhubarb¹ | Sept. 1–Oct. 1 | Sept. 15–Oct. 15 | Sept. 15–Nov. 1 | Oct. 1–Nov. 1 | Oct. 15–Nov. 15 | Oct. 15–Dec. 1. |
| Rutabaga | May 15–June 15 | May 1–June 15 | June 1–July 1 | June 15–July 15 | June 15–July 15 | July 10–20. |
| Salsify | May 15–June 1 | May 15–June 15 | May 20–June 20 | June 1–July 1 | June 15–July 1 | June 1–July 1. |
| Shallot | (²) | (²) | (²) | (²) | (²) | (²) |
| Sorrel | May 15–June 15 | May 1–June 15 | June 1–July 1 | June 1–July 15 | July 1–Aug. 1 | July 15–Aug. 15. |
| Soybean | | | | May 25–June 10 | June 1–25 | June 1–July 5. |
| Spinach | May 15–July 1 | June 1–July 15 | June 1–Aug. 1 | July 1–Aug. 15 | Aug. 1–Sept. 1 | Aug. 20–Sept. 10. |
| Spinach, New Zealand | | June 1–20 | May 15–July 1 | May 15–July 1 | June 1–July 15 | June 1–Aug. 1. |
| Squash, summer | June 10–20 | June 1–20 | May 15–July 1 | June 1–July 1 | June 1–July 1 | June 1–July 20. |
| Squash, winter | | | May 20–June 10 | June 1–July 1 | June 1–July 1 | June 1–July 1. |
| Sweet potato | | | | | May 20–June 10 | June 1–15. |
| Tomato | June 20–30 | June 10–20 | June 1–20 | June 1–20 | June 1–20 | June 1–July 1. |
| Turnip | May 15–June 15 | June 1–July 1 | June 1–July 15 | June 1–Aug. 1 | July 1–Aug. 1 | July 15–Aug. 15. |
| Watermelon | | June 1–July 1 | May 1–June 15 | May 15–June 15 | June 1–June 15 | June 15–July 20. |

¹Plants    ²Generally spring-planted

| Crop | Oct. 30 | Nov. 10 | Nov. 20 | Nov. 30 | Dec. 10 | Dec. 20 |
|---|---|---|---|---|---|---|
| Asparagus¹ | Nov. 15–Jan. 1 | Dec. 1 |  | Aug. 1–Sept. 15 | Sept. 1–30 | Sept. 1–Oct. 1 |
| Beans, lima | July 1–Aug. 1 | July 1–Aug. 15 | July 15–Sept. 15 | Aug. 15–Sept. 20 | Sept. 1–30 | Sept. 1–Nov. 1 |
| Beans, snap | July 1–Sept. 1 | July 1–Sept. 1 | July 1–Sept. 10 | Sept. 1–Nov. 1 | Sept. 1–Dec. 31 | Sept. 1–Dec. 31 |
| Beet | Aug. 1–Sept. 1 | Aug. 1–Oct. 1 | Sept. 1–Dec. 1 | Sept. 1–Dec. 15 | Aug. 1–Nov. 1 | Sept. 1–Dec. 31 |
| Broccoli, sprouting | July 1–Aug. 15 | Aug. 1–Sept. 1 | Aug. 1–Sept. 15 | Aug. 1–Oct. 1 | Aug. 1–Nov. 1 | Sept. 1–Dec. 31 |
| Brussels sprouts | July 1–Aug. 15 | Aug. 1–Sept. 1 | Aug. 1–Sept. 15 | Aug. 1–Oct. 1 | Sept. 1–Dec. 31 | Sept. 1–Dec. 31 |
| Cabbage¹ | Aug. 1–Sept. 1 | Sept. 1–15 | Sept. 1–Dec. 1 | Sept. 1–Dec. 1 | Sept. 1–Nov. 15 | Sept. 1–Dec. 1 |
| Cabbage, Chinese | Aug. 1–Sept. 15 | Aug. 15–Oct. 1 | Sept. 1–Oct. 15 | Sept. 1–Nov. 1 | Sept. 1–Dec. 1 | Sept. 15–Dec. 1 |
| Carrot | July 1–Aug. 15 | Aug. 1–Sept. 1 | Sept. 1–Nov. 1 | Sept. 15–Dec. 1 | Sept. 15–Dec. 1 | Sept. 15–Nov. 1 |
| Cauliflower¹ | July 15–Aug. 15 | Aug. 1–Sept. 1 | Aug. 1–Sept. 15 | Aug. 15–Oct. 10 | Sept. 1–Oct. 20 | Oct. 1–Dec. 31 |
| Celery¹ and celeriac | June 1–Aug. 15 | July 1–Aug. 15 | July 15–Sept. 11 | Aug. 1–Dec. 1 | Aug. 1–Dec. 31 | Oct. 1–Dec. 31 |
| Chard | June 1–Sept. 10 | June 1–Sept. 15 | June 1–Dec. 1 | June 1–Nov. 1 | June 1–Dec. 31 | June 1–Dec. 31 |
| Chervil and chives | (²) | (²) | Nov. 1–Dec. 31 | Nov. 1–Dec. 31 | Nov. 1–Dec. 31 | Nov. 1–Dec. 31 |
| Chicory, witloof | July 1–Aug. 10 | July 10–Aug. 20 | July 20–Sept. 1 | Aug. 15–Sept. 30 | Aug. 15–Oct. 15 | Aug. 15–Oct. 15 |
| Collards¹ | Aug. 1–Sept. 15 | Aug. 15–Oct. 1 | Aug. 25–Nov. 1 | Sept. 1–Dec. 1 | Sept. 1–Dec. 31 | Sept. 1–Dec. 31 |
| Corn salad | Sept. 15–Nov. 1 | Oct. 1–Dec. 1 | Oct. 1–Dec. 1 | Oct. 1–Dec. 31 | Oct. 1–Dec. 31 | Oct. 1–Dec. 31 |
| Corn, sweet | June 1–Aug. 1 | June 1–Aug. 15 | June 1–Sept. 1 | June 1–Sept. 1 |  |  |
| Cress, upland | Sept. 15–Nov. 1 | Oct. 1–Dec. 1 | Oct. 1–Dec. 1 | Oct. 1–Dec. 31 | Oct. 1–Dec. 31 | Oct. 1–Dec. 31 |
| Cucumber | June 1–Aug. 1 | June 1–Aug. 15 | June 1–Aug. 15 | July 15–Sept. 15 | Aug. 15–Oct. 1 | Aug. 15–Oct. 1 |
| Eggplant¹ | June 1–July 1 | June 1–July 15 | June 1–Aug. 1 | July 1–Sept. 1 | Aug. 1–Sept. 30 | Aug. 1–Sept. 30 |
| Endive | July 15–Aug. 15 | Aug. 1–Sept. 1 | Sept. 1–Oct. 1 | Sept. 1–Nov. 15 | Sept. 1–Dec. 31 | Sept. 1–Dec. 31 |
| Fennel, Florence | July 1–Aug. 1 | July 15–Aug. 15 | Aug. 15–Sept. 15 | Sept. 1–Nov. 15 | Sept. 1–Dec. 1 | Sept. 1–Dec. 1 |
| Garlic | (²) | Aug. 1–Oct. 1 | Aug. 15–Oct. 1 | Sept. 1–Nov. 15 | Sept. 15–Nov. 15 | Sept. 15–Nov. 15 |
| Horseradish¹ | (²) | (²) | (²) | (²) | (²) | (²) |
| Kale | July 15–Sept. 1 | Aug. 1–Sept. 15 | Aug. 15–Oct. 15 | Sept. 1–Dec. 1 | Sept. 1–Dec. 31 | Sept. 1–Dec. 31 |
| Kohlrabi | Aug. 1–Sept. 1 | Aug. 15–Sept. 15 | Sept. 1–Oct. 15 | Sept. 1–Dec. 1 | Sept. 15–Dec. 31 | Sept. 1–Dec. 31 |
| Leek¹ | (²) | (²) | Sept. 1–Nov. 1 | Sept. 1–Nov. 1 | Sept. 1–Nov. 1 | Sept. 15–Nov. 1 |
| Lettuce, head¹ | Aug. 1–Sept. 15 | Aug. 15–Oct. 15 | Sept. 1–Nov. 1 | Sept. 1–Dec. 1 | Sept. 15–Dec. 31 | Sept. 15–Dec. 31 |
| Lettuce, leaf | Aug. 15–Oct. 1 | Aug. 25–Oct. 1 | Sept. 1–Nov. 1 | Sept. 1–Dec. 1 | Sept. 15–Dec. 31 | Sept. 15–Dec. 31 |
| Muskmelon | July 1–July 15 | July 15–July 30 |  |  |  |  |
| Mustard | Aug. 15–Oct. 15 | Aug. 15–Nov. 1 | Sept. 1–Dec. 1 | Sept. 1–Dec. 1 | Sept. 1–Dec. 1 | Sept. 15–Dec. 1 |
| Okra | June 1–Aug. 10 | June 1–Aug. 20 | June 1–Sept. 10 | June 1–Sept. 20 | Aug. 1–Oct. 1 | Aug. 1–Oct. 1 |
| Onion¹ | (²) | Sept. 1–Oct. 15 | Oct. 1–Dec. 31 | Oct. 1–Dec. 31 | Oct. 1–Dec. 31 | Sept. 15–Nov. 1 |
| Onion, seed |  |  | Sept. 1–Nov. 1 | Sept. 1–Nov. 1 | Sept. 1–Nov. 1 | Sept. 1–Nov. 1 |
| Onion, sets |  | Oct. 1–Dec. 1 | Nov. 1–Dec. 31 | Nov. 1–Dec. 31 | Nov. 1–Dec. 31 | Oct. 1–Dec. 31 |
| Parsley | Aug. 1–Sept. 15 | Sept. 1–Nov. 15 | Sept. 1–Dec. 1 | Sept. 1–Dec. 1 | Sept. 1–Dec. 31 | Sept. 1–Dec. 31 |
| Parsnip | (²) | (²) | Aug. 1–Sept. 1 | Sept. 1–Nov. 15 | Aug. 1–Sept. 1 |  |
| Peas, garden | Aug. 1–Sept. 15 | Sept. 1–Nov. 1 | Oct. 1–Dec. 1 | Oct. 1–Dec. 1 | Oct. 1–Dec. 31 | Oct. 1–Dec. 1 |
| Peas, black-eyed | June 1–Aug. 1 | June 15–Aug. 15 | July 1–Sept. 1 | July 1–Sept. 10 | July 1–Sept. 10 | July 1–Sept. 20 |
| Pepper¹ | June 1–July 20 | June 1–Aug. 1 | July 1–Sept. 1 | July 1–Sept. 1 | Aug. 15–Oct. 1 | Aug. 15–Oct. 1 |
| Potato | July 20–Aug. 10 | July 25–Aug. 20 | Aug. 10–Sept. 15 | Aug. 1–Sept. 15 | Aug. 1–Sept. 15 | Aug. 1–Sept. 15 |
| Radish | Aug. 15–Oct. 15 | Sept. 1–Nov. 15 | Sept. 1–Dec. 1 | Sept. 1–Dec. 1 | Sept. 1–Dec. 31 | Sept. 1–Dec. 31 |
| Rhubarb¹ | Nov. 1–Dec. 1 |  |  |  |  |  |
| Rutabaga | July 15–Aug. 1 | July 15–Aug. 15 | Aug. 1–Sept. 1 | Sept. 1–Nov. 15 | Oct. 1–Nov. 15 | Oct. 15–Nov. 15 |
| Salsify | June 1–July 10 | June 15–July 20 | July 15–Aug. 15 | Aug. 15–Sept. 30 | Aug. 15–Oct. 15 | Sept. 1–Oct. 31 |
| Shallot | (²) | (²) | Aug. 15–Oct. 15 | Aug. 15–Oct. 15 | Sept. 15–Nov. 1 | Sept. 15–Nov. 1 |
| Sorrel | Aug. 1–Sept. 15 | Aug. 1–Sept. 15 | Aug. 15–Oct. 15 | Sept. 1–Nov. 15 | Sept. 1–Dec. 15 | Sept. 1–Dec. 31 |
| Soybean | June 1–July 15 | June 1–July 25 | June 1–July 30 | June 1–July 30 | June 1–July 30 | June 1–July 30 |
| Spinach | Sept. 1–Oct. 1 | Sept. 15–Nov. 1 | Oct. 1–Dec. 1 | Oct. 1–Dec. 31 | Oct. 1–Dec. 31 | Sept. 1–Dec. 31 |
| Spinach, New Zealand | June 1–Aug. 1 | June 1–Aug. 15 | June 1–Aug. 15 | June 15–Aug. 15 | June 1–Sept. 15 | June 1–Sept. 15 |
| Squash, summer | June 1–Aug. 1 | June 1–Aug. 10 | June 1–Aug. 20 | June 1–Sept. 1 | June 1–Sept. 15 | June 1–Oct. 1 |
| Squash, winter | June 10–July 10 | June 20–July 20 | July 1–Aug. 1 | July 1–Aug. 1 | July 1–Sept. 1 | Aug. 1–Sept. 15 |
| Sweet potato | June 1–15 | June 1–July 15 | June 1–July 1 | June 1–July 1 | June 1–July 1 | June 1–July 1 |
| Tomato | June 1–July 1 | June 1–July 15 | June 1–Aug. 1 | Aug. 1–Sept. 1 | Aug. 15–Oct. 1 | June 1–Nov. 1 |
| Turnip | Aug. 1–Sept. 15 | Sept. 1–Oct. 15 | Sept. 1–Nov. 15 | Sept. 1–Nov. 15 | Sept. 1–Dec. 1 | Sept. 1–Dec. 31 |
| Watermelon | July 1–July 15 | July 15–July 30 | June 1–July 20 | June 1–July 1 | Oct. 1–Dec. 1 | Oct. 1–Dec. 31 |

¹Plants    ²Generally spring-planted

# Getting
# an Early
# Start

If you live in an area where the vegetable gardening season is only 3 or 4 months long, it may be worthwhile to start the garden early by using a hotbed, a cold frame, or simply by starting seed in flats (shallow boxes) and setting the plants out after the danger of frost has passed.

## Using Seed Flats

You can buy seed flats at garden supply centers or make them yourself. In addition to shallow boxes, any container in which plants are grown is suitable for starting seedling plants that will be transplanted later.

Select an appropriate seed flat, and fill it with peat pots. Fill the pots with a soil mix of equal parts garden loam and peat moss, or use sterilized potting soil from the garden supply store. Sow the seed in the flat, from 1 to 5 seeds in each peat pot. Sowing 1 seed per pot is the most convenient method because you may then plant the pots directly in the ground when the time comes. If you sow several seed in a peat pot, you must remove the seedlings from the pot, and separate them before planting them in the garden. Either method has advantages; one is convenient, the other is inexpensive.

In general sow seed in flats 4 to 6 weeks before the anticipated transplanting time. Locate the flat in filtered light, and keep the soil slightly moist until the plants are set out.

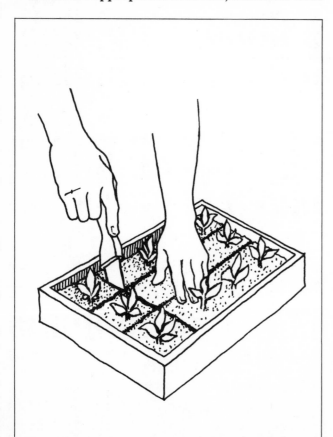

To remove seedlings from a flat, make downward slices as if you are cutting a cake; then remove each seedling with a trowel, and transplant into rows in the garden.

Fill flat with planting medium to within ¾ inch from the top; then level with hand. Use a thin, straight board the same width as the flat to make furrows.

Gently tap seeds from package as evenly as possible into the furrows. Cover seeds with additional soil, and firm with hand.

Water seeds with a fine mist or a sprinkler can to prevent washing them out of furrows.

Larger, fan-shaped leaves are cotyledons, or "seed leaves." Smaller leaves growing above them are true leaves. These plants are ready to be transplanted.

## Hotcaps and Plastic Row Covers

You can gain a week or two in the spring garden by protecting seedling plants with a cover of polyethylene plastic. Small plastic tents (called *Hotcaps*) are available commercially for covering individual plants. To cover an entire row, bend old coat hangers to form wickets over the row; then lay a sheet of polyethylene over the wickets. Use clip-type clothespins to fasten shut the ends of the tent at night. Open the ends on warm days to allow ventilation. Such covers not only raise the temperature around the plants by creating a greenhouse effect, but they also protect the seedlings from hard rains.

Clear plastic may be used to cover an entire row or individual plants. This cold protection allows earlier planting.

## Hotbeds

A hotbed is a small, enclosed, heated garden in which plants may be grown out of season. The walls of the hotbed may be made of bricks, concrete blocks, or 2-inch boards. The top may be of glass, lucite, or polyethylene plastic mounted on a wooden frame that is attached with hinges and can be raised as a lid. Heating units are available through hardware stores and garden supply centers.

Hotbeds are useful for starting flowering annuals in abundance, rooting shrubbery cuttings, overwintering tender ornamental plants, and for getting a real head start (up to 2 months) with vegetable plants.

Locate the hotbed in a sunny spot, preferably on the south side of a building, a fence, or other protective structure. Do not locate in an area subject to flooding.

### BUILDING A HOTBED

The size of the bed will depend on your needs. A convenient width is 6 feet. Since standard hotbed sash covers are usually 3 × 6 feet, convenient lengths are multiples of 3 feet, such as 6, 9, 12, or 15 feet. If you build your own sash, you can make it any size you wish. If an electric heating cable is to be used, a 6- × 6-foot bed or 6- × 9-foot bed is the usual size for the shortest heating cable available.

Materials for building beds may be formed concrete, bricks, concrete blocks, or lumber 2 inches thick. Use tongue-and-groove lumber to avoid air cracks, or put weatherstripping over the joints. Lumber that is 1 inch thick can be used, especially in the South, if soil is banked against the outside of the bed for insulation. You can use any kind of wood, but cypress and oak will not rot as quickly as other woods. Lumber may be treated to retard decay. Use a material that does not injure plants, such as copper naphthenate. **Caution: Do not use creosote or pentachlorophenol; these are toxic to plants.**

Walls made of blocks or bricks should be laid on a concrete footing. The footing should be poured 2 to 4 inches thick on a firm subsoil. Joints of blocks or bricks should be mortared, especially in the upper South; but in the lower South, a temporary frame can be made of blocks without mortar if soil is banked against the outside to seal cracks against cold winds.

Wooden frames can be nailed together, squared, and put in place after the ground is leveled. Long frames will need bracing. This bracing can be provided by driving 2 × 4s into the ground on the outside of the frame and nailing the frame to them. Soil should be banked against the outside of the frame on all sides for insulation and for draining water away from the bed. Do not leave trenches that will hold water around the bed.

The hotbed should slope to the south to get the best exposure to the light and warmth of the sun. On beds 6 feet wide, the cover should be 6 inches lower on the south side. The north wall should be 18 to 24 inches high and the south wall, 12 to 18 inches high, depending on the size of plants to be grown and soil level inside the hotbed.

The cover should fit snugly in order to conserve heat in the bed. A standard 3- × 6-foot hotbed glass sash is more expensive but will

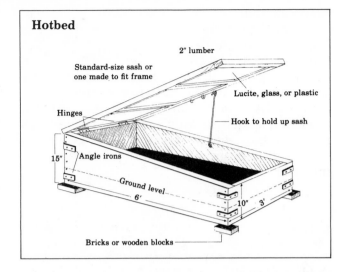

**Hotbed**

2" lumber

Standard-size sash or one made to fit frame

Lucite, glass, or plastic

Hinges

Hook to hold up sash

15"

Angle irons

Ground level

6'

10"   3'

Bricks or wooden blocks

last longer than transparent glass-substitute materials. One of the best glass substitutes is clear or translucent plastic. Fasten the plastic to sash frames for longer life and ease of removing or lifting for ventilation.

Sash frames for plastic can be made of 2 × 2s or 1 × 2s. They may be standard 3- × 6-foot size or larger since they will be lighter than a glass sash. Since plastic is somewhat elastic, rainwater may stand on the cover unless the plastic is supported by strips in the sash about 1 foot apart. In the upper South, it is best to cover both sides of the sash with plastic for better insulation. Strips of thin wood lath tacked over the plastic where it is fastened to the frame will keep it from being whipped loose and torn by wind.

HEATING UNITS

Hotbeds may be heated with heating cables or incandescent light bulbs. You can use standard lead-coated or plastic-covered soil heating cable or 25-watt, frosted light bulbs. The temperature in either type bed can be controlled with a thermostat. Light bulbs will protect plants from cold but will not heat the soil as well as a cable placed in the soil. Also, plants tend to be more spindly when the bed is heated with light bulbs.

Light bulbs should be about 10 or 12 inches above soil surface, fastened to strips of lumber or supported by non-electric wires. Allow one 25-watt bulb for each 2 square feet of bed space (position bulbs 1 to 2 feet apart). Larger bulbs may burn plants located near the bulb.

Heating cable usually comes in 60-foot lengths for a regular 115-volt electrical circuit or in 120-foot lengths for a 230-volt circuit. The 60-foot length is enough for a 6- × 6- or 6- × 8-foot bed. Cable loops should be laid about 8 inches apart for uniform heating of the soil. Do not bend cable sharply or its covering may be broken.

Cable can be laid on smooth soil in the floor of the bed unless a layer of gravel or other coarse material is needed for drainage. In this case cover coarse material with old sacks and add a 2-inch layer of sand upon which to lay the cable. After the cable is laid cover it with about 2 inches of sand or soil. On top of the sand or soil add hardware cloth or poultry netting to protect the cable from hoes, spades, or rakes

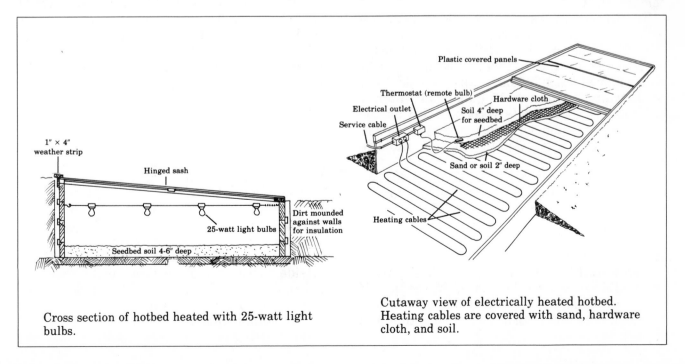

1" × 4" weather strip

Hinged sash

25-watt light bulbs

Dirt mounded against walls for insulation

Seedbed soil 4-6" deep

Cross section of hotbed heated with 25-watt light bulbs.

Plastic covered panels

Thermostat (remote bulb)

Electrical outlet

Hardware cloth

Soil 4" deep for seedbed

Service cable

Sand or soil 2" deep

Heating cables

Cutaway view of electrically heated hotbed. Heating cables are covered with sand, hardware cloth, and soil.

used in working the bed or removing plants with soil. If plants are to be started in flats or other containers, these are set on the protective netting; otherwise, soil is placed 4 inches deep on top of the netting.

A reliable soil thermometer should be used in regulating the thermostat to desired temperature and to check bed temperature during the time the bed is in use. The thermostat bulb and the thermometer bulb should be placed about 2 inches deep and midway between loops in the heating cable. If you wish to regulate bed by air temperature instead of soil temperature (especially when light bulbs are used) lay the thermostat bulb on top of the soil or insert it lengthwise so that half the bulb is above the soil surface.

Some heating cables are manufactured with a built-in 70° F. thermostat.

### SOIL FOR HOTBEDS

If your soil is mellow or loamy, it can be used without special treatment—except possibly sterilization. If the soil is too tight, it may be improved by mixing it about half and half with sand or a 2-1-1 mixture of soil, sand, and either compost, leaf mold, peat moss, vermiculite, or a peat-lite mix.

Soil, unless it has been brought in from the woods, may need fumigating to kill nematodes, soil-borne diseases, and weed seed. Soil can be treated after it is placed in a hotbed or in seed flats, but it must be covered with airtight material for 24 to 48 hours, depending on the temperature.

To kill nematodes and diseases, you can use either formaldehyde or chloropicrin (tear gas). Soil should be sprinkled with a water solution of the chemical and covered with sacks or canvas for at least 24 hours. Mix formaldehyde at the rate of 1 pint in 15 gallons of water or chloropicrin at the rate recommended on the label. Soil treated with formaldehyde should not be used to grow plants of the cabbage family.

For diseases only, such as damping-off, soil can be treated with a water solution of 4 pounds of copper sulfate (bluestone) in 25 gallons of water.

### PLANTING

Sow seed thinly in rows 4 to 6 inches apart in the bed or in a seed flat placed in the bed. If small seedlings are to be transferred to a cold frame or pots, rows can be as close together as 2 inches.

### TEMPERATURE

For prompt germination of seed and production of stocky plants, the following table gives the best temperature and the length of time normally needed to have plants ready to set. Of course plants will grow at a lower temperature (so long as they do not freeze), but they will require a longer growing time, and such plants may not be healthy or vigorous. It is best to bring soil to desired temperature before planting seed.

| Crops | Hotbed Temperature (Degrees F.) | Time Required (Weeks) |
|---|---|---|
| Cabbage family | 65 to 70 | 4 to 6 |
| Celery | 65 to 70 | 8 to 10 |
| Lettuce | 60 to 65 | 3 to 4 |
| Onions | 70 | 5 to 7 |
| Eggplants | 70 to 75 | 6 to 8 |
| Peppers | 70 to 75 | 7 to 8 |
| Tomatoes | 70 to 75 | 5 to 7 |
| Melon family | 80 to 85 | 3 to 4 |
| Sweet potatoes | 80 to 85 | 3 to 4 |

### VENTILATING THE BED

Hotbeds need some ventilation to control temperature and air humidity. On warm, sunny days it may be necessary to open or remove the cover to keep air temperature in the bed from rising above 85°. In the case of electric hotbeds, heat can be turned off during such warm days. Covers should be replaced and heat turned on again at night except when plants are being "hardened off" the last week or two before transplanting. If there is danger of frost, however, covers should be replaced at night on beds containing frost-tender crops.

### WATERING

Hotbeds should be watered often enough to keep the soil fairly moist. It is best to water beds during the morning because sunlight will warm the water and soil and save cost of heating, and soil surface will have time to dry off before night, reducing the likelihood of damping-off.

About a week or two before time to set plants in the garden, they can gradually be adjusted to outside weather (hardened off) by keeping the bed cooler and, if it is necessary to slow down growth, by reducing the amount of water. Do not let plants wilt severely, however.

When using peat pots water heavily the first

time to soak the pot. Also, just before moving plants to the garden (whether in pots or not), water them thoroughly.

It is usually best not to fertilize soil before planting seed unless the soil is prepared several days ahead of planting. Regular garden fertilizer can be used to topdress beds, but one of the soluble fertilizers sold as starter solution is ideal.

Do not overfertilize beds. It is best to fertilize lightly and repeat later if plants show a need for more. About 1 pint of garden fertilizer for a 6- × 6-foot bed is usually enough each time. Broadcast evenly when plants are dry, brush fertilizer off plants, and water thoroughly. If a starter solution is used dissolve it in water (usually 1 cupful in 5 gallons), and sprinkle evenly over the bed; then water the bed to help fertilizer penetrate the soil and to wash the leaves.

## Cold Frames

A cold frame is nothing more than a hotbed without heat. In most cases cold frames are built of inexpensive materials, such as 1-inch boards. But it is still a good practice to mound soil against walls for insulation and to drain water away from the frame. Many people construct cold frames wider than hotbeds and the same height on all sides. This construction is fine if plants are in pots, flats, or other contain-ers. But if plants are set out in soil in the frame, it's easier to pull them if beds are not more than 6 feet wide.

The cover can be any protective fabric; a transparent material such as plastic is preferred. Plastic can be fastened to the sash, as for the hotbeds, or rolled on and off in large sheets. In the latter case, the frame should have no rough, sharp corners to tear the material.

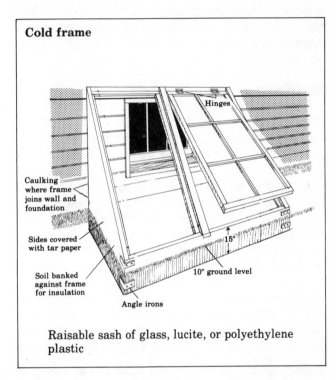

**Cold frame**

Hinges

Caulking where frame joins wall and foundation

Sides covered with tar paper

Soil banked against frame for insulation

Angle irons

15″

10″ ground level

Raisable sash of glass, lucite, or polyethylene plastic

# Routine Garden Care

Keeping your plants healthy and productive requires daily care throughout the growing season. Routine activities include irrigating, weeding, fertilizing, harvesting, and controlling pests and diseases. Failure to attend to weeds in the garden can result in crop loss, but there are some methods that can cut down considerably on the time and effort you must spend.

## Mulching

The greatest time- and energy-saving technique is mulching. To mulch means to spread a covering material on the garden between the plants and between the rows of plants (i.e., anywhere garden plants are NOT growing). Materials commonly used for mulching include hay, pine straw, grass clippings, rotted leaves, compost, and black polyethylene plastic.

Mulch stabilizes soil temperature, allowing earlier planting and later harvesting; it cuts off sunlight from weeds and seriously hampers their growth, and it conserves moisture in the soil by slowing down evaporation. In dry areas of the country a mulched garden has a 100 percent greater chance of surviving than does an unmulched one. Other effects of mulching

Mulch spread on the ground around plant stems controls weeds and retains soil moisture. Common mulch materials include grass clippings (shown here), pine straw, hay, shredded leaves, black plastic, and a number of other materials.

The soil around these bush beans has been disturbed to show a mulch of old fertilizer bags just beneath the surface. Covering unsightly mulches with soil or organic mulch improves the appearance of the garden.

Even an old, discarded rug can be used as mulch. Cut holes in the rug, then set plants or plant seed through the holes.

include protecting plants from splattering caused by pelting rain; discouraging the spread of fungus diseases by preventing splattering; providing a "mat" for vegetables to lie on, thereby discouraging rot; and improving soil structure by retarding compaction. An added benefit is that the mulch can be tilled into the soil at the end of the season to further improve soil structure and fertility. In sloping gardens mulch prevents soil erosion during heavy rains.

There are also disadvantages to mulching, depending on the material used: hay mulch may contain seeds that could become weeds next year or the year after; clippings of common Bermudagrass can root and become weeds; mulch offers a hiding place for mice, moles, cutworms, and other small pests; mulches left on the garden during the rainy Southern winter can become a harboring place for disease organisms. But these seem easier to cope with than constant weeding, fruit rotting on the ground, and the worry of too much or too little rain.

Each of the above problems can be averted. The importation of weed seed to the garden has been exaggerated. The soil already contains weed seed (some seed can live in the soil for 15 or 20 years before germination), and new weeds that do arise can be kept under control by adding more mulch. Pine straw, shredded bark, sawdust, and other mulch materials contain no weed seed. Traps can be set for the few rodents that might become a problem. And fungus diseases may be avoided by either tilling the mulch into the soil in the fall or by gathering the mulch and adding it to the compost pile.

Composting will also kill much of the ungerminated seed in hay.

In small gardens, the best time to mulch is after tilling, before you begin to plant. Cover the entire garden with mulch 2 to 4 inches thick, depending on the material (e.g., 2 inches of sawdust or 4 inches of hay). When you are ready to plant part the mulch where you want to dig seed rows, and plant seed. When the plants reach a height of 4 to 6 inches tuck the mulch snugly against the stems. Be sure to mulch the middles of the rows (i.e., between plants as well as between rows) as this is where weeds will be hardest to eliminate if they are allowed to grow.

Mulch may be applied to a garden at any time after the plants are 4 to 6 inches high. Spread the mulch first in the paths between the plant rows, then work it in around the stems of the plants. Apply mulch after a rain or after watering the garden, but do not mulch a dry garden.

The finer the mulching material, the more readily it will decompose. The microorganisms in the soil that cause decomposition may become competitors for the nitrogen, which your plants depend upon for nutriment. To avoid a nitrogen deficiency, broadcast 4 pounds nitrate of soda or 10 pounds cottonseed meal per 100 square feet (10 × 10 feet) of area mulched. With sawdust, mix 1 pound nitrate of soda or 1/2 pound ammonium nitrate with each bushel of sawdust before applying the sawdust to the garden. (It takes 5 to 7 bushels of sawdust on 100 square feet of surface to make a mulch 1 inch deep.)

## BLACK PLASTIC MULCH

Black plastic sheeting is also used as a mulch. Plastic should be 1½ mils thick and 3 or 4 feet wide and is available at most nurseries. Black plastic controls weeds, holds moisture in the soil, and reduces spotting of fruits and pods. Do not use clear plastic; weeds will grow under it.

Because dark colors absorb heat, black plastic is especially good for early planted crops. The soil is 5° to 10° warmer under the plastic. Crops come up faster and mature faster, sometimes as much as 3 weeks earlier than normal. During the summer, however, the soil may get too warm under the plastic. This may be overcome by spacing plants close together, so that they shade the soil. Further shade may be provided by laying paper or cardboard over the plastic in spots that are particularly exposed to sunlight. If you are mulching an established garden, lay the plastic between rows and mulch the spaces between the plants with sawdust or fine straw. Fine materials allow better penetration of water.

The best time to apply black plastic mulch is before planting.

1. A double row method, by which a single sheet of plastic is used to cover two rows, is good.
2. Cut rows of holes 2½ inches in diameter through which seed may be sown or plants set. Space the holes according to the requirements of the particular vegetables you will be growing. You may also use a long-handled bulb planter to punch the holes in the plastic.
3. In the spaces between the planting holes make T-shaped slits about 3 feet apart to allow water to pass through to the soil. The stem of the T should point in the direction from which the water flows. In gardens which slope make the watering slits closer together, depending on the degree of the slope.
4. Fertilizer can be dissolved in water and applied through the watering slits.

**Black Plastic Mulch**

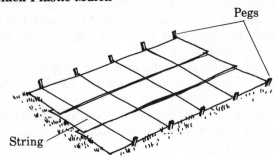

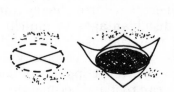

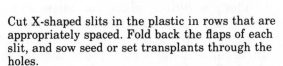

Lay sheets of black plastic over the entire garden. Sheets should overlap a few inches. Anchor plastic with pegs and string or rocks.

Cut X-shaped slits in the plastic in rows that are appropriately spaced. Fold back the flaps of each slit, and sow seed or set transplants through the holes.

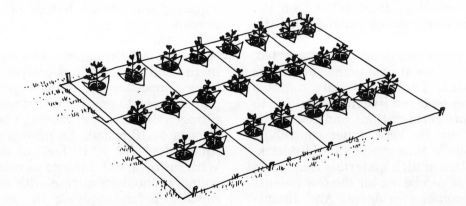

As plants grow, tuck plastic around stems to control weeds. Punch holes in the spaces between rows to allow rainwater to penetrate.

Cement blocks provide support and add a note of interest to this garden. Note that the pine straw mulch is parted to reveal a mulch of black polyethylene plastic.

## Irrigating

Irrigating and mulching the garden can help to assure good vegetable production regardless of drought and heat. A small irrigating system, large enough to water a sizable home garden properly, is not very expensive; if your garden is level enough for furrow or seepage irrigation, cost will be even less. You may easily save enough in increased vegetable production in a year or two to pay the entire cost of installation.

A perforated sprinkler or a soaker hose may be run down the middle of each row. This method is especially good because it doesn't allow leaves to become wet. Wet leaves encourage the spread of fungus diseases. You can make a soaker hose from an old, leaky hose. Block off one end with a rubber cork; then punch holes along the sides of the hose at 12-inch intervals.

Sandy soils will not hold as much moisture as heavier soils or those soils with plenty of humus. During prolonged drought, plants on sandy land may need about an inch of water every 5 to 7 days; heavier soils need about 1¼ to 1½ inches of water every 7 to 10 days, depending on the size of plants and the temperature. Water plants thoroughly when watering becomes necessary. Deep watering encourages plants to develop long, sturdy roots.

Some crops such as lima beans, cucumbers, Southern peas, okra, peppers, Irish potatoes, and sweet potatoes are more resistant to drought than others. Sweet corn will stand more drought with less damage while plants are small than if the drought comes while the plants are silking and tasseling. With any crop, however, best results come when plants are never allowed to suffer from lack of moisture.

Mulching is not a complete substitute for irrigation, but it will greatly reduce damage from drought.

## Weed Control

Weeds, not insects and diseases, are the number one enemy of vegetable gardens. Weeds rob plants of sunlight, moisture, nutrients, and growing space. In addition, some weeds may attract destructive insects which will spread to the garden plants. Weed control, then, is a crucial garden concern.

A weed, by definition, is a plant that causes determent to the cultivated crop or disfigure-

During dry spells, the garden will need watering. Use a soaker hose or a sprinkler, as shown here.

ment to the place where it is growing. This definition alone suggests the best method of dealing with this pest: removal. If you pull weeds by hand, pull up as much as possible of the root system. Otherwise, the roots will produce new top growth, and you'll be pulling the same weed in a week. In small gardens hand pulling and mulching are the best methods of weed control. Mulching doesn't eliminate weeds completely, but it leaves very few and keeps the soil among them loose enough to permit easy removal by hand.

### Stakes and Trellises

Some plants are easier to care for and to harvest if they are given support. Tomatoes, pole beans, black-eyed peas, and cucumbers all respond well to this type of culture. Staked plants are easier to protect against weeds, drought, and insect pests. In addition, staked plants take up a minimum of space.

Nearly any sturdy, upright rod or pole can be used as a stake. Garden supply centers often stock precut stakes. The length of the stakes varies with the region. In the North, tomatoes seldom grow higher than 3 or 4 feet, whereas in the South, tomatoes may reach 9 to 10 feet. Select stakes according to the anticipated

height of the plants you intend to stake.

A simple trellis can be made with posts and clothesline rope. Drive two 4-inch diameter posts into the ground 10 feet apart. The height of the posts, like the height of stakes, will depend on the anticipated height of plants. A cucumber trellis need be no more than 2 to 4 feet high, but tomato and pole bean trellises should be as high as 8 feet in areas with a long growing season. Post holes should be at least 2 feet deep.

The bottom rope between the two posts should be 2 feet above ground; the second rope, 4 feet above ground; the third rope, 6 feet above, and so on. For pole beans and black-eyed peas, two horizontal supports are enough (one rope near the top and one 6 inches above ground). Tie string vertically between the two ropes for the vines to climb.

Chicken wire and chain link fences also provide support for beans, black-eyed peas, English peas, cucumbers, and lima beans.

Not only do trellises make gardening easier, but also they can be used as living screens to give the garden a neatly bordered, enclosed feeling.

Erect stakes and trellises at planting time or shortly thereafter.

For best production, stake your tomato plants. Staked plants are easier to care for and easier to harvest. An added advantage is that they require less space.

Pole beans must have support, or they become a tangled mess. The vines can twine around the strings of this trellis allowing easier care, easier harvest, greater yield, and early insect or disease detection. Trellised pole beans also take very little space.

A trellis of chicken wire provides excellent support for cucumbers. Planted in front of the trellis, the vines will climb the chicken wire. Trellising conserves space, increases exposure of fruits to sun, and makes pest control easier.

## Fertilizing

With repeated use of compost (or manure) and green manure cover crops year after year, the soil may accumulate too much nitrogen. In such cases vegetables grown for their roots or tubers, such as potatoes, will need only phosphate and potash. Furthermore, too much nitrogen tends to cause fruit-bearing vegetables, such as tomatoes, to produce abundant vegetative growth but only a few fruits. This does not mean that you should eliminate the use of compost (or manure) and legume cover crops, but it does mean that plant food that is not supplied by these materials should be added. Apply phosphate and potash when fall cover crops are planted or when compost is added. Use about 1,000 pounds phosphate and 300 pounds muriate of potash per acre (or about 1,200 pounds of 0-14-14).

Even where there is an abundance of organic nitrogen in the soil, nitrogen fertilizer as a side-dressing (1/4 pound of ammonium nitrate, or 1/2 pound of sodium nitrate or ammonium sulfate per 100 feet of row) in early spring is worthwhile because it is in a form plants can use immediately. When the soil is cool, organic nitrogen is not converted very rapidly to the forms used by plants.

### APPLYING FERTILIZER

Vegetables that are not well fertilized will not give good yields and will lack quality, vitamins, and food elements. As was mentioned in Chapter One, "Planning and Preparation," a complete fertilizer should be applied to the garden about 2 weeks before scheduled planting. Make light applications of fertilizer every 2 or 3 weeks until the plants reach maturity. The following are common methods of applying fertilizer.

- *Banding fertilizer.* Make small furrows 2 to 3 inches to either side of the seed row, and sprinkle a band of fertilizer on the bottom. Use 5 to 8 pounds of a complete fertilizer per 100 feet of row. Make the fertilizer furrows deep enough so that the fertilizer is on a level 2 inches below the level of the seed. Cover the bands with soil. Fertilizer can then leach (filter) slowly down into the root zone of the soil.
- *Side-dressing.* Side-dressing is the application of fertilizer on the surface of the soil after plants have begun to grow. Either sprinkle it along plant rows or, in fertilizing hill plantings, apply a circle of fertilizer around the hill. Apply the fertilizer no

**Banding Fertilizer**

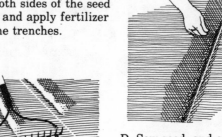

A. Mark off the seed row with stakes and string; dig trenches with a hoe on both sides of the seed row, and apply fertilizer in the trenches.

C. Use a hoe to dig a seed row between the refilled trenches.

B. Rake soil back over the fertilized trenches.

D. Sow seed, and cover it. As the seedling plants begin to grow, their roots will spread into the fertilized areas.

Side-dressing means sprinkling fertilizer along a row of plants.

closer than 6 or 8 inches to the plants, and never apply fertilizer when the plants are wet. Use a fine spray of the garden hose to wash the fertilizer into the soil.

## FERTILIZER DOSAGE AND APPLICATION SCHEDULE

Vegetable plants vary in their fertilizer requirements. Cabbage and tomatoes need considerably more fertilizer than do green beans or Southern peas. The following chart will give you an idea of the relative fertilizer requirements of common vegetable plants.

In the absence of a soil test, vegetables in the Heavy Feeders column should receive about 25 pounds of 10-10-10 or 6-12-12 per 1,000 square feet as an initial preplanting dosage to be applied 2 to 3 weeks before planting. Beginning about 1 month after plants are up and thriving make regular light applications of complete fertilizer every 2 weeks. About 1 cup of fertilizer per 50 feet of row is sufficient.

For medium feeders, apply 15 to 20 pounds of complete fertilizer per 1,000 square feet as a soil preparation. Make routine applications of 1 cup of fertilizer per 75 feet of row every 2 to 4 weeks.

In preparing soil for light feeders mix in fertilizer at the rate of 8 to 10 pounds of complete fertilizer per 1,000 square feet. During the growing season make 2 or 3 additional applications, using 1 cup of complete fertilizer per 150 feet of row.

## NITROGEN FERTILIZER

Vegetables that consist of vegetative matter should receive 1 or 2 supplementary doses of nitrogen fertilizer such as ammonium nitrate (about 35% N) or ammonium sulfate (20% N) during the growing season.

Vegetative plants (leaves or stems are edible portions) include mustard, collards, spinach, chard, lettuce, and turnip greens. The portion of the plant we eat is the best clue as to what kind of fertilizer to use in routine applications made during the growing season. The edible portion of tomatoes, beans and okra is the fruit (be sure the fertilizer contains potassium). The edible portion of corn and peas is the seed (use potassium). The edible portion of cabbage, broccoli, cauliflower, and head lettuce is the flower or flower bud (also needing potassium), and the desirable portion of carrots, beets, parsnips, and radishes is the root (use fertilizer containing phosphorus, potassium, and nitrogen).

| *Heavy Feeders* | *Medium Feeders* | | *Light Feeders* |
|---|---|---|---|
| *10-10-10 or 6-12-12* | *10-10-10 or 6-12-12* | | *6-12-12* |
| *1,500–1,700 pounds/acre* | *800–1,000 pounds/acre* | | *400 pounds/acre* |
| Cabbage | Artichokes | Herbs | Southern Peas |
| Celery | Asparagus | Okra | |
| Irish Potatoes | Beans (all types) | Peas, English | |
| Lettuce | Beets | Peppers | |
| Onions | Cantaloupes | Pumpkins | |
| Sweet Potatoes | Carrots | Radishes | |
| Tomatoes | Corn, Sweet | Rhubarb | |
| | Cucumbers | Swiss Chard | |
| | Eggplants | Watermelons | |
| | Greens (kale, collards, mustard, turnips, broccoli, cauliflower, spinach) | | |

# Controlling Garden Pests

The first step in controlling insects, diseases, and other damaging pests is learning to recognize the enemy. The "Garden Pest Control Chart" at the end of this chapter will help you identify pests and suggest ways of controlling them.

Good sanitation, rotation, and care of crops will go a long way in preventing trouble with garden pests.

**Cultural Practices**

Get into the habit of caring for your garden. The care you show will bring a bountiful harvest. The following is a list of good cultural practices:

- Locate and arrange the garden properly. When possible select an area that is well drained. Rotating the garden to a new location every few years will help with nematode control.
- Rotate crops within the garden so that the same vegetable does not occupy the same area year after year. This will help in controlling soil-borne diseases, such as wilt on tomatoes and melons.
- Fumigate soil if necessary. To control root knot and other nematodes, weeds, and soil-borne diseases, it may be necessary to fumigate, especially if you must use the same garden location year after year. With continuous land use, fumigation is the best solution for such nematode susceptible crops as tomato, okra, beans, cucurbits (cucumbers, squash, cantaloupes, watermelons), and other taprooted crops.
- Fertilize correctly. Use ample fertilizer and lime as indicated by soil test. For example, adequate lime in the soil will help reduce blossom-end rot on tomatoes. Use enough fertilizer to keep plants moderately vigorous.
- Use good seed of adapted varieties. Many disease-resistant varieties of vegetables have been introduced in recent years and, where adaptable, these varieties should be selected for growing.
- Buy disease-free seed and plants.
- Thin young plants to avoid overcrowding. This will allow better air circulation and thorough coverage with dust or spray materials when needed.

- Avoid handling plants when they are wet. Cultivating and harvesting while the plants are wet often spread bacterial disease spores.
- Water the garden soil when needed, but try not to get the plants wet. Best times to water are early morning and late afternoon. Water applied during peak hours of sun may be lost through evaporation. If you water in the later part of the day, do it early enough so that the water will not stand in the garden overnight. This encourages mildew and damping-off, a fungus disease which causes seedlings to rot near soil level.
- Tobacco mosaic, a virus that is often present in manufactured tobacco products, may be spread to tomatoes, peppers, and eggplants if the handler has just used tobacco. Wash hands thoroughly with soap and water before working these crops. Remove any plants that are affected by mosaic (dwarfed plants with dark green, mottled leaves, which are often twisted or distorted), and avoid handling healthy plants after handling plants diseased with mosaic.
- Cucumber mosaic is a virus disease that can be spread by first handling diseased plants and then handling healthy ones. The disease is also spread by such insects as aphids (plant lice) and cucumber beetles; therefore, the control of these insects is important in controlling mosaic and bacterial wilt disease.
- Insect damage is less likely where weeds are not allowed to flourish. Weeds may harbor certain virus diseases and insects (such as aphids and cucumber beetles) that spread virus diseases. Weeds also interfere with thorough dusting or spraying of garden crops.
- Some insect damage (wireworms, rootworms, white grubs) is more likely to occur in soil that has been grassy. These insects are likely to appear in areas that have been converted from lawn to vegetable plots.
- Thorough preparation of land at least 3 weeks before planting seed will reduce the likelihood of damage by certain insects.
- Planting as early as the weather permits will often allow the crop to mature before

serious insect populations build up.

- Harvesting produce as soon as it matures will shorten the amount of time during which it is susceptible to insect damage.
- Destroy old plants. Plow old plants under as soon as each crop has finished bearing. This will stop the buildup of insects and disease spores that will attack later plantings. Plow out plant roots, and leave them exposed to the sun for a few days to help destroy nematodes. Then plow under roots and tops, and let them rot.

### Protection Against Birds

In some areas, birds will eat newly planted vegetable seed right out of the ground. Many protective measures have been employed over the centuries. The scarecrow is one of the most proven. Some gardeners report that setting plastic snakes in the garden scares the birds away. Another old practice is to grow catnip near the garden to keep cats in the area.

Small gardens are easier to protect than large gardens. Seed rows may be covered with plastic netting or with chicken wire. The latter method is especially useful in areas of high rainfall. The chicken wire may be covered with a thin layer of mulch during storms to protect seedlings from pelting rain.

Chicken wire covers for seed rows keep the birds away from newly planted seed.

Some gardeners have used light-reflecting metal wind chimes to deter the birds. Strips of aluminum foil hung here and there in the garden will accomplish the same end.

No one method will work for more than a few days at a time. Alternate methods as the birds regain their courage.

Milk carton "collars" protect young tomato plants from cutworms, slugs, and rodents. After plants are set out, place sections of milk cartons over them.

### Insects and Diseases

The adage "An ounce of prevention is worth a pound of cure" is particularly appropriate to insect and disease control.

The organic approach as discussed in Chapter Nine, "Organic Vegetable Gardening," can be tried before resorting to "chemical warfare."

But if insects or diseases threaten to take over your garden, spray or dust with pesticides. *Insecticides are used to control insects.* Watch for insects; if they begin to multiply, apply insecticide. *Fungicides are used to control certain plant diseases.* Fungus diseases, which infect leaves and fruits, spread most rapidly during damp weather. This is the most critical time to keep plants covered with a protective coating of fungicide.

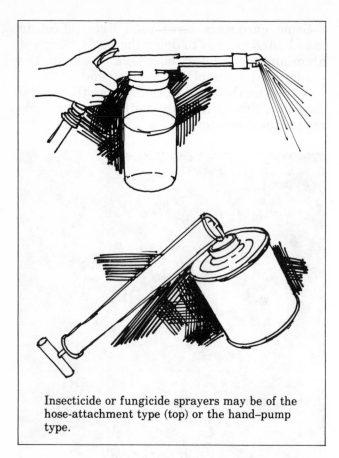

Insecticide or fungicide sprayers may be of the hose-attachment type (top) or the hand–pump type.

### HOW TO APPLY PESTICIDES

Insecticides are usually sold as dusts, emulsifiable concentrates, or wettable powders. Dusts are applied directly to the foliage of plants. Emulsifiable concentrates are first dissolved in water, then applied as sprays. If you buy either of these spray-type insecticides be sure to purchase a spray bottle or other spraying device.

Spraying is generally more effective than dusting. Most destructive garden insects attack the undersides of leaves. Sprays can be applied to both surfaces whereas dusts are applied only to the top surfaces. The insect must then chew a hole in the foliage in order to be affected by the insecticide.

Fungicides are applied as sprays or soil drenches, depending on whether the destructive fungus is an aerial organism or a soil organism.

Nematocides (used to kill nematodes) are usually applied as soil drenches since most nematodes that attack vegetables are soil-borne.

Read pesticide labels, and follow directions judiciously. Federal and state regulations prohibit exceeding label recommendations. Imprudent application can do more harm than good.

Always store pesticides in a safe, dry place, out of the reach of children and pets.

Avoid applying insecticide to the entire garden at one time. This inevitably kills all the beneficial insects. Use insecticides that break down rapidly as opposed to those with strong residual effects. This means that after the insecticide has broken down, beneficial insects can move back into the area. Carbaryl (Sevin), malathion, and rotenone will control most vegetable garden insects and break down completely in 2 to 5 days.

The "Garden Pest Control Chart" tells you what insects and diseases look like and what chemicals are effective in controlling them. The trade names of the recommended chemicals follow in the "Pesticide Identification Guide."

Spray the undersides of leaves as well as the upper surfaces. Most insects attack the undersides.

| Crop | Pest | Look For | Control Measure |
|---|---|---|---|
| ASPARAGUS | Asparagus Beetle | Bugs with red, black, and yellow markings that feed on tender shoots and leaves. | Dust or spray with methoxychlor up to 3 days of harvest; rotenone, carbaryl, or malathion up to one day of harvest. |
| | Rust | Orange yellow blisters on shoots. | Plant resistant varieties. |
| BEANS, Snap and Lima | Mexican Bean Beetle | Lacy appearance caused by bugs feeding on underside of leaves; yellow, fuzzy larvae and copper-colored spotted beetles. | Dust or spray with carbaryl or rotenone up to and during picking; malathion up to one day of picking; or methoxychlor up to 3 days of picking. |
| | Bean Leaf Beetle | Holes eaten in leaves. | Same control as for Mexican bean beetle. |
| | Corn Earworm | Holes eaten in pods. | Same control as for Mexican bean beetle. |
| | Anthracnose | Reddish brown spots on stems and leaves. | Use Western-grown seed; do not work plants or pick when wet; rotate crops. |
| | Bacterial Blight | Dark or reddish brown spots on leaves, stems, and pods. | Same control as for anthracnose. |
| | Bean Mosaic | Plants stunted, leaves mottled and distorted; caused by a virus. | Plant resistant varieties. Use Western-grown seed; control sucking insects, especially aphids. |
| | Downy Mildew of Lima Beans | White mold on pods; may also kill leaves and blossoms. | Spray or dust with zineb or maneb every 7 days. |
| | Rust | Rusty spots that spread during humid weather. | Plant resistant varieties. Dust with finely powdered sulfur every 7 days. |
| | Root-Knot Nematodes | Swellings on roots, stunted plants. | Rotate. Treat soil with Nemagone or Fumazone before planting. |
| | Stem and Root Rot | Reddish brown lesions or rot on stem near or below soil line. The entire root system may be rotted. Affected young plants appear stunted and off-colored and may slowly die. | Rotate. Plant certified, disease-free seed. |
| CABBAGE, BROCCOLI, CAULIFLOWER, BRUSSELS SPROUTS, COLLARDS, KALE, TURNIPS, MUSTARD GREENS | Cabbage Looper (worms) | Green worms; holes eaten in leaves. | Dust or spray every 7 to 10 days with endosulfan or malathion; methoxychlor up to 2 weeks of harvest; bacillus thuringiensis until 1 day of harvest; rotenone during harvest. |
| | Harlequin Bugs | Bugs that suck sap or juices from plants. | Dust or spray with malathion up to 7 days of harvest; sabadilla dust to 1 day of harvest. Handpick bugs and egg masses. |
| | Black Rot (of cabbage) | | Rotate. Buy healthy plants. |

| Crop | Pest | Look For | Control Measure |
|------|------|----------|-----------------|
| | Yellows (of cabbage) | A fusarium wilt disease. Plants that turn yellow and drop leaves. | Rotate. Plant resistant varieties. |
| | White Leaf Spot | Circular spots help to distinguish this disease from similar turnip leaf spots of anthracnose or downy mildew. The latter spots are more irregular. | Dust or spray with maneb every 5 to 7 days. |
| | Downy Mildew | Yellowish, angular spots on older leaves, fruits not affected. Leaves dry, curl, and die. | Apply a dust or spray with maneb or zineb. Grow mildew-resistant varieties. |
| | Cabbageworms | Feed on underside of leaves, producing ragged holes; bore into heads. | Control same as for cabbage looper. |
| | Cross-Striped Cabbageworms | Caterpillars are gray when they first hatch. They later have tiny black stripes across the bluish gray back and a bright yellow stripe along each side. They riddle the heads and tender buds of cabbage and other cole crops with holes. | Control same as for cabbage looper. |
| CUCUMBERS, SQUASH, CANTALOUPES, WATERMELONS, PUMPKINS | Cucumber Beetles | Striped and 12-spotted beetles that feed on leaves, stems, and blossoms; start on young seedlings. | Dust or spray with malathion up to 1 day of harvest (3 days on pumpkin); methoxychlor up to 7 days; rotenone or carbaryl any time. |
| | Pickleworms and Melonworms | Whitish to green, slender worms that bore into fruit and buds. | Dust or spray with malathion up to 1 day of picking; methoxychlor, up to 7 days; carbaryl any time. Start at bloom and put on every 7 days. |
| | Squash Bug | Bugs that cluster on leaves and runners, suck sap from plants. | Malathion, methoxychlor, or carbaryl as for cucumber beetles; or sabadilla dust. Handpick bugs. |
| | Anthracnose | Dead spots on leaves and cankers on fruit; worse on watermelons. | Plant resistant varieties. Treat seed. Dust or spray with zineb or maneb. |
| | Bacterial Wilt | Sudden wilting and dying of plants; spread by cucumber beetles. | Control cucumber beetles. Remove infected plants from garden. |
| | Cucumber Mosaic | Mottled, curled leaves; warty fruit. | Since disease is spread by aphids, control aphids with malathion up to 1 day of harvest. |
| | Downy Mildew | Spreads fastest during damp, humid weather. | Spray or dust plants thoroughly every 7 to 10 days with zineb, Captan, or copper fungicide. Plant resistant varieties. |
| | Leaf Spots | Dead spots on leaves; older leaves attacked first. | Plant treated seed. Dust or spray as for downy mildew. |
| | Nematodes | Swellings or knots on roots. Stunted plants. | Rotate. Fumigate soil before planting with a nematocide, such as Nemagon or Fumazone. |
| | Alternaria Blight | Causes direct damage to leaves and stems. The fungus survives mainly on old cantaloupe refuse but may also survive and be carried on seed. | Control same as for anthracnose. |

| Crop | Pest | Look For | Control Measure |
|------|------|----------|-----------------|
| | Gummy Stem Blight | Causes direct damage to stems and leaves. Excessive damage causes considerable reduction of yields and quality of fruits. | Spray or dust with maneb or zineb. |
| | Fusarium Wilt | Stunted seedlings; wilted vines; reduced yields. Plants eventually die. | Grow wilt-resistant varieties. |
| | Fruit Rot | Brown and shrunken stems at soil line; brown or gray spots on leaves; large, ringed, circular, tan, or brown spots covered with small blisters on fruits. | Grow rot-resistant varieties. |
| | Squash Mosaic | Yellow spots on leaves and, occasionally, on fruits; stunted plants; reduced yields. Most common on straightneck and crookneck summer squash. | Remove and destroy diseased plants and perennial weeds. Follow controls for cucumber beetle. |
| | Squash Scab | Sunken, dark brown spots on fruits. Gummy substance oozes from fruits. In moist weather, spots are covered by grayish olive fungus growth. Some small, brown spots on leaves and stems. Damage worse in cool, moist weather. | Do not grow squash in same soil more often than once in 3 years. Best control is to spray or dust every 3 days with maneb. |
| | Squash Beetle | Both the squash beetle and its larva gnaw away the under surface of the leaf. The upper surface of the leaf shrinks away from the intact veins and the damaged area looks lacy. | Spray or dust with carbaryl. |
| | Powdery Mildew | Direct damage is to leaves, which eventually become yellow. | Dust or spray with dinocap at the first sign of disease. |
| | Belly Rot | Damage is to the side of the cucumber in contact with soil. These fungi may also cause damping-off and seedling damage to many plants. | Rotate crops. |
| CORN, Sweet | Corn Earworm | Worm feeding in tips of ears. | Dust or spray silks with carbaryl. Begin when silks first appear and repeat every 2 to 3 days until silks turn brown. |
| | European Corn Borer | Worms tunneling into stalks and ears. | Start dusting with carbaryl or diazinon as soon as damage is noticed in whorl; repeat three or four times if necessary. |
| | Billbug | This is a weevil or "snout" beetle. A crust of soil over the body hides this insect's grayish brown to black color. Neat, straight rows of small holes across the leaves of surviving plants identify leaves that were fed upon before they unroll. Leaves may be ragged. | Control same as for corn earworm. |
| | Sugarcane Beetle | Hard, shiny, black beetles about 1/2 inch long eat ragged, gaping holes in corn stalks just below the ground. | Control same as for corn earworm. |

| Crop | Pest | Look For | Control Measure |
|------|------|----------|-----------------|
| | Seed-Corn Maggot | Yellowish white; legless; 1/4 to 1/3 inch long. Bores into sprouting seed and prevents development of plants. | Plant insecticide-treated seed and plant in warm weather. Replant immediately if maggot damage is heavy. |
| | Fall Armyworm | Worms are green, pinkish, light tan, or nearly black. They have a white upside down "Y" on their dark brown heads. They cause ragged holes in the leaves. | Apply a dust or spray containing carbaryl or naled to grasses and weeds around the garden and to foliage in the garden that is not to be eaten. |
| | Wireworms | Yellow to white with dark heads and tails; slender; 1/2 to 1 1/2 inches long when full grown. Resembles a jointed wire. | Treat soil with diazinon before planting. |
| | Rootworm or Budworm | Rootworms damage corn in the same way as wireworms. Rootworms are the larvae of the cucumber beetle. | Control same as for wireworms. |
| | Smut | Large, irregularly shaped white galls, or outgrowths, form on stalks, ears, and tassels. Galls burst, releasing masses of black fungus spores. Fungus lives in soil. | Remove and destroy galls. Do not use diseased plants in making compost. |
| | Southern Cornstalk Borer | This dirty grayish white caterpillar is conspicuously marked with many dark brown spots. It grows to about 1 inch long as it bores within the stalk and bud. Damaged corn plants are usually twisted and stunted. Leaves are sometimes ragged from holes that were chewed out when the leaf was still rolled up in the bud. | Control same as for European corn borer. |
| LETTUCE | Lettuce Drop | Wilting of outer leaves, watery soft rot on stems and old leaves; wilted and decayed plants. Disease worse in moist weather. | Avoid close planting and poorly drained soil. Ridge soil slightly about plants to prevent water from accumulating. |
| ONIONS, SHALLOTS | Thrips | Tiny, yellow or black, active insects that rasp leaves and suck juices, causing whitish blotches. | Dust or spray with malathion up to 3 days of harvest. Carbaryl or toxaphene can be used if tops are not to be eaten. |
| | Neck Rot and Leaf Spot | Damage to leaves in garden or decay of bulbs after harvest. | Rotate. Do not bruise or overexpose to sun when harvesting. Let crop mature before harvest. |
| OKRA | Corn Earworms, Aphids, Cabbage Loopers, Stinkbugs | Chewing and sucking insects. | Handpick insects. Dust or spray with carbaryl before pods form; malathion up to 3 days of harvest; sabadilla to 1 day of harvest; carbaryl for worms any time. |
| | Nematodes | Damage to roots such as "knots"; stunted plants. Okra is very susceptible. | Fumigate soil with Nemagon or Fumazone. |
| | Wilt | Stunted plants; lower leaves that turn yellow and drop off. | Root damage by nematodes lets wilt enter plant. Control nematodes. |

| Crop | Pest | Look For | Control Measure |
|---|---|---|---|
| PEAS, English or Garden | Aphids | Small, greenish insects that suck sap, distort tender growth and pods. | Spray or dust with malathion up to 3 days of harvest. |
| | Bacterial Blight | | Plant Western-grown seed. Treat seed. |
| | Seed Decay and Root Rot | Poor stand; yellowing of leaves. | Rotate. Plant certified seed. |
| PEAS, Field, Cowpeas, or Southern Peas | Bean Leaf Beetle | Holes eaten in leaves. | See beans. |
| | Cowpea Curculio | "Wormy" peas caused by adult weevil stinging pods and laying eggs. | Apply methoxychlor or toxaphene dust or spray 3 or 4 times at three-day intervals beginning when the first blooms appear. Do not apply after pods form. |
| TOMATOES, EGGPLANTS, PEPPERS, IRISH POTATOES | Colorado Potato Beetle | Feeding on foliage. | Spray or dust with carbaryl. |
| | Flea-Beetles | Tiny holes in leaves where beetles feed. | Spray or dust with carbaryl or malathion. |
| | Hornworms | Feeding on foliage. | Use carbaryl or toxaphene. Wash fruit at harvest. |
| | Leafhoppers | Small, slender, greenish hoppers that suck sap, cause edges of leaves to turn brown and curl. | Spray or dust with carbaryl, malathion, or methoxychlor. Wash residue from fruit at harvest. |
| | Tomato Fruitworm | Holes eaten in fruit; same insect as corn earworm. | Spray or dust with carbaryl every 7 to 10 days after fruits set. |
| | Bacterial Spot | Leaves having small, yellowish spots with dark centers. | Plant certified seed that are free from diseases. |
| | Blossom-End Rot | Black, leathery rot on blossom end of fruits or pods. | Lime soil. Mulch to keep even moisture in soil. |
| | Early Blight | Irregular brown spots on leaves (spots have "concentric rings" inside); starts on older leaves. Spots or rot on shoulder of fruit next to stem. More trouble in warm, damp weather. | Spray or dust plants thoroughly every 7 to 10 days with maneb, zineb, Captan, or copper fungicide. Repeat after rains to keep plants protected. |
| | Late Blight | Leaves having irregular greenish black spots with pale green border; white mold on lower surface. Rapid spread in cool, damp weather. | Spray as for early blight. Buy certified, disease-free seed or plants. Some Irish potato varieties are resistant to late blight. |
| | Tomato Mosaic | Leaves twisted or puckered, mottled color; stunted plants. Same virus causes tobacco mosaic. | Avoid unnecessary handling of plants. Do not use tobacco while working in these crops; wash hands with soap and water. Control weeds and insects. |
| | Nematodes | Stunted plants; roots that are swollen or knotty. | Rotate. Fumigate soil. |

| Crop | Pest | Look For | Control Measure |
|---|---|---|---|
| | Wilts | First symptom—wilting and yellowing of lower limbs or leaves. Infection through roots moving up stems, tissue just under "bark" turning brown. Sudden wilting of entire plant; caused by bacterial wilt. Pith of stems clogged and "water soaked." | Plant tomato varieties resistant to fusarium wilt—none is resistant to bacterial wilt; or, use soil sterilant-type chemical (see chemical weed control section this chapter). For bacterial wilt, avoid low, poorly drained soil. Also worse on newly cleared land. |
| | Irish Potato Scab | Rough, scabby, raised or pitted spots on tubers. | Plant clean tubers. Do not grow potatoes in soil where disease has occurred. Do not use lime, woodashes, or fresh stable manure on soil where potatoes are to be grown. Grow scab-resistant varieties. |
| | Gray Leaf Spot | Round brown spots with gray centers that occur on leaves. Spots are smaller than those of early blight. | Remove or turn under vines in the fall. Destroy perennial weeds. Rotate crops. Apply a dust or spray containing a fixed copper or organic fungicide. |
| | Leaf Miners | Larvae make long, slender, winding, white tunnels in the leaves of tomato, pepper, and spinach. The larva is yellow and is about 1/8 inch long. | Apply a spray containing diazinon or dimethoate. |
| | Southern Blight | Distinguishing sign is white mold present on infected stem near soil line. This fungus also causes rot of tomato and other plant parts in contact with soil. The fungus lives in the soil for many years. | Deep plowing to bury all residue in bottom of furrow will help. Rotate with grass crop. |
| SWEET POTATOES | Flea Beetles, Tortoise Beetles, and Sweet Potato Leaf Beetles | Damage to leaves, mostly small holes. | Dust or spray with endosulfan as needed. |
| | Sweet Potato Weevil | Shiny, antlike, slender snout beetle; legs and middle body bright red. Young grub bores into roots and stems. Very destructive in parts of Lower South. | Plant certified, weevil-free seed, slips, or vine cuttings. Contact County Agent or your state department of entomology for control recommendations and regulations. |
| | Wireworm | Shallow holes in fleshy roots. Larvae of flea beetles, leaf beetles, and other insects may also cause this damage. | Apply diazinon granules to the foliage when roots begin to enlarge. Plant on land that was clean cultivated the previous year. |
| | Black Rot, Scurf, Internal Cork, Wilt or Stem Rot, or other diseases | Surface rots or scabby areas on fleshy roots; corky tissue inside potato; stunted, wilted, or yellow plants. | At least 3- to 4-year rotation; plant only certified, disease-free seed, plants, or vine cuttings. |
| ANY CROP | Ants | Nests or mounds built in garden. Often spread aphids. | Rake mounds to open them. Pour boiling water over ants. |
| | Aphids (plant lice) | Tiny, greenish insects that suck plant juices, cause distorted growth; spread diseases, too. | Spray or dust plants with malathion (see label for days from last application to harvest for each crop). |

| Crop | Pest | Look For | Control Measure |
|------|------|----------|-----------------|
| | Blister Beetles | Brightly colored beetles working mostly in droves. Especially bad on eggplant, tomatoes, and Irish potatoes. | Dust or spray with carbaryl or toxaphene, except on cucumbers, melons, etc. (Use malathion on these or any crop close to harvest. See label for how close to harvest each may be used.) |
| | Cutworms | | Wrap paper collar around stem of transplanted plant. Treat soil around plant base with carbaryl, diazinon, or toxaphene. |
| | Damping-Off | Sudden wilting, falling over, and dying of young seedlings. | Plant on raised bed for good drainage. |
| | Green Stinkbug | Large, green, shield-shaped bug that sucks plant juices; causing ill-shaped fruit, pimples, or "cloudy spots." | Dust or spray with carbaryl before edible parts form; or sabadilla up to 1 day of harvest. |
| | Japanese Beetles | Shining metallic green, oval, ½ inch long beetles that feed on many plants; larvae feed on roots. | Dust or spray with carbaryl before edible parts of plants form; later use methoxychlor or malathion (see label for how close to harvest these may be used on different crops). Soil insecticides also help. |
| | Spider Mites ("red spider") | Tiny red or greenish mites that suck juices from underside of leaves. Leaves with webbing on underside and faded color. | Dust or spray with dicofol, diazinon, or malathion until 1 to 7 days (see label) of harvest, depending on crop. |
| | Seed-Corn Maggots | Poor stands caused by destruction of corn, bean, and pea seed after planting. More trouble in cool, wet soil. | Plant only after the soil has warmed up and use seed that has been commercially treated with an insecticide. |
| | Vegetable Weevil | Small grayish brown adult or light green grubs that feed on leaves and roots of turnips and other crops, mostly in cool weather. | Use malathion dust or spray up to 3 days of harvest on turnips (see label for other crops). |
| | White Grubs and Wireworms | Damage to underground parts of plants. | Treat soil with diazinon. |

| Common Name | Chemical Name | Trade Names |
|---|---|---|
| Bacillus Thuringiensis | | Agritol, Bakthane, Biotrol, Dipel, Larvatrol, Thuricide, Tribactur |
| Captan | N-(trichloromethylthio)-4-cyclohexene-1, 2-dicarboxmide | Merpan, Orthocide 406 |
| Carbaryl | 1-Naphthyl N-methylcarbamate | Hexavin, Karbaspray, Ravyon, Septene, Sevin, Tricarnam |
| Diazinon (ISO, BSI) | 0, 0-Diethyl 0-(2-isopropyl-6-methyl-4-pyrimidinyl) phosphorothioate | Basudin, Diazajet, Diazide, Diazol, Dazzel, G-24480, Gardentox, Spectracide |
| Dimethoate | 0,0-Dimethyl S-(N-methylcarbamoylmethyl) phosphorodithioate | Cygon, Daphene, De-fend, Fostion MM, Perfekthion, Rogor, Roxion, Trimetion |
| Dinocap | 2-(1-Methyl-n-heptyl)-4,6-dinitrophenyl crotonate, with its isomer 4-(1-methyl-n-heptyl)-2,6-dinitrophenyl crotonate | Arathane (former name), Iscothane, Mildex |
| Endosulfan | 6,7,8,9,10,10-Hexachloro-1,5,5a 6,9,9a-hydro-6,9-methano-2,4,3-benzo(e)-dioxathiepin-3-oxide | Chlorthiepin, Cyclodan, Hoe 2671, Insectophene, Kop-Thiodan, Malix, Thifor, Thimul, Thionex, Thiodan |
| Malathion | 0,0-Dimethyl Phosphorodithioate of diethylmercaptosuccinate | Cythion, Emmatos, Fyfanon, Karbofos, Kop-Thion, Kypfos, Malaspray, Malamar, MLT, Zithiol |
| Maneb | Manganese ethylene-1,2-bis-dithiocarbamate | Chloroble M, Dithane M-22, Dithane-Manganese, Kypman 80, Maneba, Manesan, Manzate, Manzate D, MEB, MnEBD, Sopranebe, Trimangol, Trimanzone |
| Methoxychlor | 1,1,1 Trichloro-2,2-bis(p-methoxyphenyl) ethane | Marlate |
| Toxaphene | Chlorinated camphene (content of combined chlorine, 67–69%) | Alltox, Clor Chem T-590, Phenacide, Phenatox, Strobane-T, Toxakil |
| Zineb | Zinc ethylene-1,2,-bis-dithiocarbamate | Aspor, Chem Zineb, Dithane Z-78, Hexathane, Kypzin, Lonacol, Pamosol 2 Forte, Parzate C, Polyram Z, Tiezene, Tricarbamix, Triofterol, Zebtox, Zidan, Zinosan |

# Growing Vegetables

For regional gardening information, contact the Agricultural Extension Service in your state (the addresses for each of the 50 state Extension Services follow in the Appendix). The service can provide you with recommended varieties charts and planting guides. Choosing the best vegetable varieties for your area of the country will prove wise at harvest time. The planting guides are full of information: spring planting dates, fall planting dates, distance between rows, distance between plants, depth to plant, and days to maturity.

Don't forget to plant flowers in the vegetable garden. Here, marigolds are grown with tomatoes. Other suitable flowers include dwarf zinnias, nasturtiums, and petunias. Try chrysanthemums and pansies in the fall and winter garden.

## How to Grow Each Vegetable

ARTICHOKES   Artichokes can be grown from either seed or suckers. The home gardener will probably find it most convenient to purchase shoots or suckers from a nursery. Artichokes need a deep, well-drained fertile soil and an abundance of fertilizer and organic matter. Avoid soils with known nematode infestations. Artichokes need a sunny location, but will require at least a half day of shade in hot areas. Set plants or suckers so that the new leafy shoots are just above ground, 4 feet apart in rows 4 to 5 feet apart.

Harvest artichokes when the buds are 2 to 4 inches in diameter by cutting 1½ inches below the base of the bud. When the plant has given its last artichoke, the stem will appear to fold up. When this occurs, cut the stem or stalk back to its base. New shoots will grow from the base. One planting of artichokes will usually produce for 4 years.

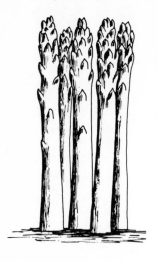

ASPARAGUS Fertile soil is a necessity for growing asparagus. It is a cool-season crop that does well in all but the southernmost regions of the Gulf states. Plants will not reach maturity for 2 years (if started from cuttings) to 3 years (if started from seed) but, once established, will continue to produce for 15 years or more.

Because asparagus occupies the ground for such a long time locate the rows to one side of the garden. Asparagus may be planted in beds, but the row method is easier to care for. Pulverize the soil and plant crowns in rows 4 to 5 feet apart. Dig the furrow or trench 10 to 12 inches deep and 24 inches wide—wide enough so that roots can be spread out in their natural position. When digging put topsoil on one side of the row and subsoil on the other.

Put 2 inches of compost or manure in the bottom of the trench or furrow. On top of this spread 10 pounds of commercial fertilizer (8-8-8, 10-10-10) for each 100 feet of row. Mix compost and fertilizer thoroughly with the soil; then cover with an inch or two of topsoil. Plant rust-resistant varieties. Set the crowns 12 to 24 inches apart, and take care to spread the roots in their natural position. Clip off any broken or injured roots, and cover the crowns with 3 inches of topsoil. Wait until after growth starts in the spring, and gradually work in enough soil to make the row level.

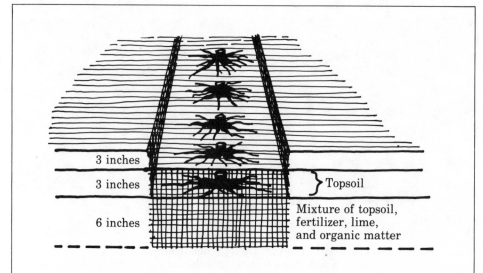

3 inches

3 inches — Topsoil

6 inches — Mixture of topsoil, fertilizer, lime, and organic matter

Trench method of planting asparagus crowns. Dig trenches 12 inches deep; fill with 6 inches of good soil and organic matter. Set crowns about 15 inches apart, and barely cover them. The filled trench should be about 3 inches lower than the surrounding soil.

Soon after the plants start growing the first season side-dress with 6-8-8 (or comparable analysis fertilizer). Use 5 to 10 pounds per 100 feet of row, and apply fertilizer on both sides of the row. In late spring side-dress with 1 pound of nitrogen fertilizer per 100 feet of row. Because asparagus does best in a neutral or slightly alkaline soil, some gardeners have found it necessary to add lime at 4- to 5-year intervals.

Do not harvest asparagus the first season. During the second season cut for only 2 to 3 weeks to allow a strong root system to develop. The spears are ready to cut when they are 6 to 8 inches long. Cut at ground level or 1½ inches below. Consider using an especially designed asparagus knife to avoid possible damage to the new shoots developing below.

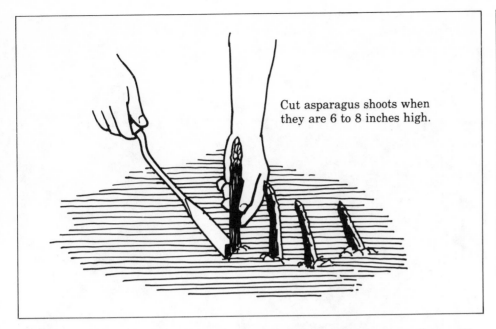

Cut asparagus shoots when they are 6 to 8 inches high.

From the third year on extend the cutting season 2 to 3 weeks until a maximum of 8 to 10 weeks is reached. Then let tops grow for the rest of the season. Each fall when the stalks die cut them to ground level, and rake and dispose of the cuttings. Then liberally broadcast a mixture of compost (or manure) and 5 to 10 pounds of 6-8-8 per 100 feet of row.

Mulch to protect roots from frost and to control weeds.

BEANS    Beans can be divided into two general groups: the low-growing (bush beans) and the tall-growing (pole beans). Beans grow well in warm weather in fertile, well-drained, thoroughly prepared soil.

Plant as soon as the danger of frost has passed. For bush varieties make rows 2½ to 3½ feet apart. Plant single seed 2 to 3 inches apart, or if the hill method is used, plant 2 or 3 seeds every 6 inches. Plant seed 1 inch deep on heavy or stiff soils and, 1½ inches deep on light or sandy soils. The depth of planting is important because beans cannot push

A trellis of stakes and strings set against a wall gives the impression that these pole beans are growing right up the wall.

Bush beans are easy to grow, easy to harvest, and easy to cook. They bear about 6 weeks after planting and continue to produce for 3 or 4 weeks, if the plants are harvested regularly.

The pods of these wax beans are purple.

their way through the soil if they are planted too deep. Plantings can be made at 2-week intervals from early spring to about 8 weeks before first frost is due.

Cultivate to kill weeds and grasses as soon as they appear, but do not cultivate or harvest when plants are wet because this often spreads diseases.

Plant pole beans after the danger of frost has passed, and locate them on one side of the garden or group with other tall-growing crops to prevent the shading of low-growing vegetables on either side.

Plant hills 12 to 24 inches apart in rows 3 to 4 feet apart, and put 2 to 4 seeds in each hill. If seed are planted much thicker than this, the vines will become so dense that rust disease may become a problem. A second planting during the summer is desirable.

Half-runners can be grown without staking or trellising but will produce better on some kind of support.

Stake or trellis pole beans when they start to run. Single stakes can be used for each hill, but teepees give the best support, especially when erected between parallel rows. Poles for single stake or teepee should be 8 feet tall and pushed 6 inches into the ground. Seed should be sown 2 or 3 at a time at the base of each pole.

Pole beans can also be sown along a fence, wall, trellis, or interplanted with corn so that cornstalks can provide support.

Seeds of beans, peas, and melons are easy to collect and carry over for planting the following year. Shown here are seeds of watermelon, black-eyed peas, purple hull peas (still in pods), and pole beans. The seeds should be dried for a few days, then stored in air-tight jars until planting time.

BUTTER BEANS Butter beans can be grown as bush limas (low-growing) or pole limas (tall-growing). Bush limas are grown in the same general way as bush beans, but they are not planted as early.

Make the first planting as soon as the danger of frost has passed and the soil has warmed up. Make plantings every 3 to 4 weeks through early July. Plant seed 1 inch deep on heavy soils and, 1½ inches deep on light or sandy soils. Plant 1 seed every 3 or 4 inches in the row, or plant 4 or 5 seeds in hills 12 inches apart.

Pole lima beans (or running butter beans) should be planted like pole beans and can be trellised in the same manner as pole beans. Rows should be 4 feet apart. Space hills 18 to 24 inches apart, and plant 2 to 3 seeds in each hill.

Many people consider the quality of the pole lima to be better than that of the bush type. However, pole limas do not bear as early as the bush limas, so you will need to plant bush limas if you desire an early crop.

Butter beans are susceptible to bean beetle damage.

BEETS Beets are easy to grow when given a start in deep, fertile, nematode-free soil. Beets are grown for their leaves as well as their roots. Many of the cultural practices recommended for beets are also good for carrots and turnips.

Soak beet seed in water overnight before planting to encourage rapid germination. Beets will withstand frost and light freezes, so plant the seed in early spring as soon as the ground is workable. Sow 15 to 18 seeds per foot of row ½ inch deep. (Make second and third plantings during the early and late summer.) When shoots are up and growing, thin to one plant every 2 to 3 inches. (Thinnings may be planted elsewhere or cooked. These young, tender greens are delicious.)

The crop maturing in late fall may be left in the ground until late freezes occur. Mound dirt against the plants, and apply additional mulch for cold protection. If indoor storage is a must, a dry place with a temperature of 50° is best.

Beets are subject to boron deficiency. If they appear stunted or develop brown heart, add to fertilizer 1 to 1½ tablespoons of household borax per 100 feet of row. A soil analysis will determine whether the soil needs lime.

BROCCOLI  Broccoli, a member of the cabbage family, is a cool-weather crop. It does best when brought to maturity in early spring and from late fall to early winter. It may be started from seed or from plants.

The spring crop should be started from plants either grown in a hotbed, cold frame, or purchased from a nursery. Place plants 12 to 18 inches apart in rows 2 to 3 feet apart. Cultivate, fertilize, and handle broccoli as you would cabbage. (For more information, see "Cabbage" in this chapter.)

The fall crop may be planted like the spring crop or started from seed that have been sown ½ inch deep, 6 inches apart in rows 2 feet apart. When plants are several inches tall, thin to 1 plant every 1½ to 2 inches.

Cut broccoli with about 5 inches of stem when it is well formed but before flower buds start to open. Keep broccoli cut to keep it producing.

BRUSSELS SPROUTS  Brussels sprouts are closely related to cabbage. Because Brussels sprouts need a cool, moist soil, they are difficult to grow in the lower South, and only a fall crop is recommended.

Plant seed ¼ inch deep in rows 2½ feet apart, and thin young plants to 1 plant for each 1½ to 2 inches. Or you may start from plants that are placed 18 inches apart in rows 2½ feet apart. Follow the same cultural practices recommended for cabbage. (For more information, see "Cabbage" in Index.) Be sure plants get enough water during the growing season.

To speed sprout maturity remove terminal bud when stalks are 12 to 14 inches high. Brussels sprouts are picked from the bottom of the stem up after they are firm and at least half the size of a golf ball. Break off the lower 8 or 10 leaves when sprouts are maturing, and continue removing 3 or 4 more leaves per week, always working from the bottom up. This gives more room for sprouts to form and directs the plant's energy to vegetable rather than to excess leaf production.

CABBAGE  Cabbage requires a sunny location and a fertile soil that is neutral or slightly alkaline. A soil pH of 6.5 to 8.5 is ideal. Start seed in a hotbed or seed flat about 6 weeks before the last killing frost is expected.

Set out plants only after the danger of frost has passed. Cabbage plants require some space: set plants of early varieties 18 to 30 inches apart. If you are planting during hot, dry weather water the seed row before sowing seed or setting plants.

Time plantings of cabbage to avoid maturing during extremely hot weather, or cracked heads may result. Head splitting may also be due to irregular watering. Be sure that cabbage plants get plenty of water on a regular schedule. Root pruning will also serve to prevent cracking heads. Simply twist the head in place a quarter turn to break some of the roots.

Cabbage plants are heavy feeders and require regular fertilization.

When preparing the cabbage seedbed broadcast 10 pounds of 8-8-8 per 100 feet of row. Mix 1 tablespoon of household borax per 10 pounds of fertilizer to avoid a boron deficiency in the soil. A starter solution (for more information, see "Making and using starter solutions" in Chapter Two, "Planting the Garden") will help newly set plants become established quickly. After growth begins side-dress with nitrogen fertilizer at the rate of 1 pound per 100 feet of row. When the leaves begin to bunch for heading side-dress them again with nitrogen at the same rate.

In cooler areas, the leaves may flower and start to go to seed rather than bunch into heads. This is called "bolting." Extended periods of temperatures below 55° may cause this. Mulch cabbage plants with 2 to 4 inches of hay for protection when cool temperatures are predicted.

Early varieties are ready for harvest in 13 to 18 weeks (from seed), and late varieties are ready in 18 to 21 weeks (from seed). Cabbages may be heavily mulched and left in the ground until early winter. Thereafter, store them in a cool, dark place.

Cabbageworms, harlequin bugs, and nematodes are among the more serious enemies of cabbage (For more information see Chapter Five, "Controlling Garden Pests.") A cardboard collar around the stem of the plant will help control cutworms. Make the collar wide enough to come up to the lower leaves. Clubroot, caused by nematodes, can be controlled by interplanting French marigolds among the cabbage plants.

CHINESE CABBAGE   Chinese cabbage is more sensitive to transplanting than cabbage, although young plants may be moved to the garden with care when the soil is warm enough to be worked. Start seed in a hotbed or cold frame about 5 weeks before the last killing frost of spring is expected. It will bolt to seed, however, if allowed to mature in hot weather.

Though Chinese cabbage is not related to cabbage, planting and fertilizing procedures are much the same. Wet the seed row before setting plants or sowing seed. Space plants 15 to 20 inches apart in rows 2½ to 3 feet apart.

Chinese cabbage needs rich soil and plenty of sun and water. Apply about 10 pounds of complete fertilizer per 100 feet of row in preparing the seedbed, then side-dress every 4 to 6 weeks with nitrogen fertilizer at the rate of 1 pound per 100 feet of row.

When the heads are firm and well developed (about 80 days from seed), Chinese cabbage is ready to harvest. You may use the leaves as well as the heads. Cut them close to the ground.

CARROTS   Carrots do best as a cool-season crop planted in sandy, loamy soil in a sunny spot. Early spring, 4 to 6 weeks before the last frost, and late summer are the best times to plant carrots.

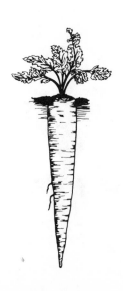

Carrot seed are slow to germinate, but there are several things you can do to encourage germination: be sure you have fresh seed; soak seed in water overnight before planting; plant radish seed along with carrot seed (radishes germinate quickly), but pull radishes up as soon as carrot tips appear, or they will interfere with carrot growth; be sure to sow seed in soil that is kept moist throughout the germinating period.

Because carrots are long-rooted, a deeply pulverized soil is necessary. If your soil is heavy, you will have to loosen it to a depth of 8 to 10 inches so that carrot roots can grow straight down. Soil should be free of roots and clods and contain no fresh manure. (Any of these factors can cause carrot roots to split.) You can grow shorter varieties if your soil is especially heavy, or try the sand trench method and grow any variety.

Sow 3 or 4 carrot seeds to the inch, 1/2 inch deep in rows 1 foot apart. As soon as plants are a few inches high thin to 1 plant every 2 to 2 1/2 inches. To promote rapid growth, side-dress with commercial fertilizer, (5-10-10 or 4-12-12).

Mulch the planted seed row 1/2 inch thick with hay, leaf mold, peat moss, or well-rotted manure to retain moisture. Water the seedlings with a fine spray as needed during hot, dry weather. As plants grow, increase the layer of mulch up to 4 inches.

CAULIFLOWER  Cauliflower cannot survive in even partially dry soil.

Grow cauliflower as a spring or fall crop by starting seed in a hotbed or by purchasing plants from a nursery.

When setting plants place them 2 1/2 to 3 feet apart in rows 3 feet apart. If you grow your own plants from seed sow them 1/4 to 1/2 inch deep. Set transplants in holes that have been soaked with water or fertilizer starter solution, and gently firm soil around the base of the plant. Cauliflower will need frequent attention. You will have to sprinkle it daily if the weather gets hot, and combine this procedure with deep soaking of the soil as it is needed. Cauliflower needs room to grow. Keep plants thinned so they are no closer than 1 1/2 feet in rows 2 feet apart. As heads start to form, pull the outer leaves over the head, and tie with string. This promotes blanching (whitening) and protects the head from the sun.

Harvest cauliflower when the head is 5 to 6 inches across and forms separate distinguishable sections.

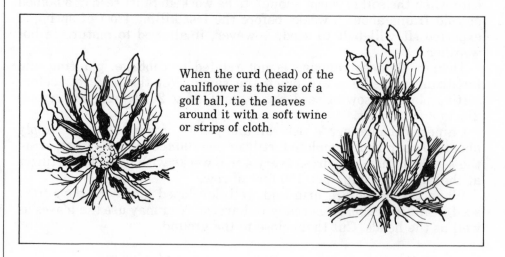

When the curd (head) of the cauliflower is the size of a golf ball, tie the leaves around it with a soft twine or strips of cloth.

CELERIAC  Celeriac is often a neglected vegetable that serves as an excellent substitute for celery and is less difficult to grow. Sometimes called "root celery," celeriac is grown for its roots rather than its stalks. Like celery, celeriac needs rich, finely pulverized soil and plenty of sun and moisture.

Planting and culture are the same as for celery, though less space is needed between rows because celeriac is not blanched.

Harvest anytime after the portion of the stem closest to the ground becomes at least 2 inches thick. Store in sand, as you would celery, or apply a thick mulch for winter protection, and dig the plants as they are needed.

Celeriac is susceptible to boron deficiency. A soil test to determine liming and fertilizing needs is strongly recommended. Household borax mixed with fertilizer can be applied to correct boron deficiency. Use 1 to 1½ tablespoons of borax with 10 pounds of fertilizer per 100 feet of row. Test the soil first as too much boron is as harmful as too little.

CELERY  Celery is grown as a fall crop in most areas of the South because it grows poorly in heat; in mountainous and other cool areas, it can be grown as a spring crop and takes about 5 months from seed.

Sow seed on a well-prepared bed that contains an ample amount of organic matter. Rich soil is a must for celery. A seed flat is best for starting celery seed because it is then possible to regulate sun and water conditions. Cover the flat with moist burlap after seeding, and remove the burlap after the seeds sprout. It takes about 2 months for the plants to grow large enough to set out. They should be at least 4 inches high. Set plants 6 inches apart in rows 2 to 3 feet apart in deep, very fertile soil that has compost or dried manure mixed in. Regular watering and regular application of a liquid fertilizer solution are necessary to grow celery. Apply fertilizer every 15 to 20 days. As the plants grow, mound dirt up around the stalks for added support. Mulch with sawdust or finely chopped hay to conserve moisture and to control weeds. If you prefer to cultivate, keep the celery bed completely free of weeds.

Though the value of blanching celery is dubious, many gardeners prefer to blanch (whiten) the plants for a week or two before harvest. This is done by cutting off sunlight from the stalks by walling the rows with 12-inch boards or placing cardboard or newspaper collars around the stalks.

Celery stores well in sand in a cool, dry place, such as a root cellar. Or, in milder sections of the country, mound dirt high against the stalks, cover the plants with hay or other light mulching material, and dig the stalks as needed.

CHARD, SWISS  Swiss Chard, a member of the beet family, makes a good spinach substitute and can be served cooked or raw as a salad

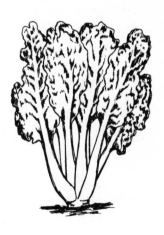

'Rhubarb' variety of Swiss chard grows larger than most varieties. Chard is the most heat-tolerant of the leafy greens and can be grown and cooked like spinach.

green. It can withstand heat and drought better than most summer greens and grows back quickly after being cut.

Sow seed heavily ½ inch deep in rows 18 inches wide. Soon after plants are up thin to one plant every 3 to 4 inches. Use the thinnings for greens. Thin again when plants begin to crowd, and leave one plant every 9 to 12 inches. Keep outer leaves cut, and chard will produce for many months.

COLLARDS   Collards are perhaps the most nutritious of green vegetables. They are also among the hardiest; a light frost even improves their flavor. They need no protective mulch until the temperature drops to 10° or 15°.

The early crop should be planted when early cabbage plants are set. Collards are more popular as a fall and winter vegetable, however.

Prepare the ground, and fertilize collards as you would cabbage. You may set plants thickly in the row, 5 to 8 inches apart, to grow into small, bunchy plants like kale, or you may set them 18 to 24 inches apart and allow them to produce large stalks. Collards may also be grown from seed, maturing in 75 days.

If you are planting during hot, dry weather water the seed row before you sow seed or set plants. This will assure more rapid germination and establishment of roots.

Collards need regular watering. Use a lawn sprinkler when rain is sparse. Water plants deeply to encourage long, healthy roots.

As the plants grow, they should be thinned to about 1 foot apart. Use the thinnings for transplanting elsewhere, for cooking, or for salad greens.

CORN, SWEET   Corn is a warm-weather crop and should be planted at the earliest safe date. Plant additional corn at two-week intervals for a continuous fresh supply.

Corn seed should be planted in soil that has been prepared with a complete fertilizer, 5-10-10. You can use either the row or hill method. Rows should be 3 feet apart, seed 1 inch deep, and plants thinned to 9 to 12 inches apart when they show above ground. Hills should be 3 feet apart on all sides. Sow 6 to 7 seeds in each hill, and, when seedlings appear, thin to 3 per hill.

To insure pollination by the wind, plant several (at least four) short rows of corn rather than one or two long ones.

Harvest corn when it is at its milky stage. Test for this by peeling back some of the husk and piercing it with your thumbnail. If the juice is milky white, corn is ready. For top quality, corn should be eaten within an hour of picking before the sugars (tender stage) turn to starch (tough stage).

CORN SALAD OR FETTICUS   Corn salad or fetticus is most valuable as a fresh green. Sometimes called lamb's lettuce, it is planted, cultivated, and used like lettuce.

Sow seed in fall, and thin plants to 6 inches apart. Corn salad matures in about 6 weeks. Make successive plantings every 2 weeks.

Corn salad needs regular watering. Side-dress with a light application of complete fertilizer once a month. Shallow cultivation is recommended to avoid damaging roots.

Corn was first grown by the Indians of North America. Today it is one of the most important crops in the world. Full sun and rich soil render the heaviest yield.

**Cucumbers** Cucumbers need a lot of watering as the fruits themselves are 96% water. Water-starved cucumbers tend to be bitter.

Plant after the danger of frost has passed. Cucumbers like a fertile, sandy soil but are less particular than most vegetables. Prepare the seedbed by digging compost (or manure) and complete fertilizer (8-8-8 or 5-10-10) into the seed rows 15 inches deep. Use 10 pounds of fertilizer per 100 feet of row. Cover this with topsoil (so that the seed is not in direct contact with the fertilizer), and sow seed 1 inch deep. For the hill system, place 5 to 7 seeds in each hill. As the plants develop, thin to the best 2 or 3 plants. Using the row method of planting, unsupported plants should be sown 12 inches apart with 5 feet between rows. Trellised cucumber plants may be grown in rows $2^{1}/_{2}$ to 3 feet apart. Side-dress with a nitrogen fertilizer every 4 to 6 weeks at the rate of 1 pound per 100 feet of row.

To make an effective trellis drive stakes a foot into the rows every 10 feet. Tie coarse string between the stakes about a foot above the ground. The stakes, consequently, should be about 5 or 6 feet long. Train the vines on the trellis to facilitate spraying and harvesting. Dwarf varieties may be grown in hanging baskets.

Cucumbers may be harvested anytime after they are 2 or 3 inches long. To extend the productivity of the plants, never allow the fruit to ripen on the vine, even if you have to pick some to throw away.

Don't be startled if cucumber leaves wilt on hot days: it's normal. Check to be certain the soil is moist under the surface.

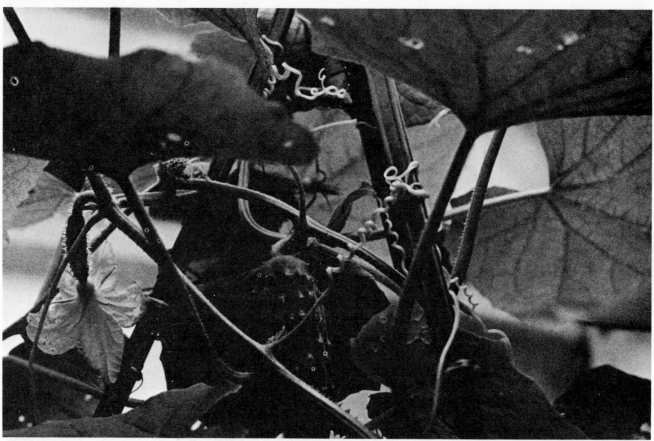

Note the coiled tendrils by which the cucumber vine climbs its support.

Chinese cucumbers form long, slim fruits rather than the stouter fruits of more common varieties.

EGGPLANT Eggplant is a heat-loving plant that grows about 2 feet tall, requires little room, and serves as a container-grown ornamental plant as well as a garden plant. Related to tomatoes and peppers, eggplant grows well in the same type soil and demands the same fertilization and watering. Three to five plants will supply enough fruit for the average family.

Start seed in a hotbed or window box. Seed requires 3 to 4 weeks to germinate. Transplant to a cold frame about 2 weeks before the time to set them out. If you prefer, you may buy plants at a nursery.

Wait until the average daily temperatures are in the high 60s and low 70s to set plants out in the garden. They are quite tender, and 2 or 3 nights of 40° or cooler may kill them. A protective mulch is recommended when cool temperatures are forecast. Set plants 3 to 4 feet apart in rows 3 to 4 feet apart.

Keep eggplants healthy and vigorous by regular watering, and side-dress them with a complete fertilizer every 4 to 6 weeks.

Eggplants are at their best when they are the size of a fist or a softball. They should reach maturity 10 to 11 weeks after being set out. Heavily fruiting plants should be staked or given other support.

Principal threats to eggplants are Colorado potato beetle and flea beetles. (For more information see Chapter Five, "Controlling Garden Pests.")

ENDIVE Endive is a good lettuce substitute and will stand more heat and grow faster in cold and rainy weather than lettuce. Curly-leaved endive is also called chicory.

Plant seed for fall crop in late summer; plant spring crop when beets and radishes are planted. Sow seed ½ inch deep, and when seedlings appear, thin to 1 plant every 15 inches. To reduce bitterness, blanch endive when leaves are dry (to prevent rotting) and heads are well developed. Blanch by tying tops of plants together with string.

The culture for lettuce and endive is similar.

GARLIC Garlic is related to the onion; culture for the two is similar. Both have been used for centuries as repellents against rodents, insects, and late blight on tomatoes and potatoes. Many gardeners use garlic tea as a spray to control aphids, white flies, and other vegetable pests. Garlic also helps control rodents in fruit orchards.

Garlic needs fertile, finely pulverized soil, and a sunny location. Divide the bulbs into individual cloves, and plant the cloves 1 to 2 inches deep. They may be interplanted with other vegetables or planted in rows. Plant them about 4 inches apart in rows 1 foot apart.

Garlic matures in 90 days. When the tops fall over, they are ready to harvest. Tie the bulbs in bunches, and hang them in a cool, dry place.

Fertilize garlic as you would onions. (For more information, see "Onions" in this chapter.)

Garlic is hardy; cold-damaged tops will grow back again.

To make garlic tea for spraying use 2 grated cloves per gallon of warm water, or use 1 teaspoon of garlic powder (found in the spice section of your grocery store) per gallon of water.

KALE Kale is a hardy green vegetable that may be planted in late winter for spring greens, but fall planting is better. The winter crop should be planted about 60 days before first frost.

Where soil is quite fertile, kale may be planted by the broadcast method, but the row method is better. Plant seed ½ inch deep in rows just as you would cabbage, and thin to 1 plant every 20 inches. The only cultivation needed is to keep down weeds and grasses and to break dry, crusty soil. (Mulching will accomplish these aims also.) Surplus plants from thinnings may be eaten or transplanted elsewhere.

Harvest kale either by cutting outer maturing leaves (this method keeps plant producing longer) or by cutting the entire plant at one time; the latter method is best if you wish to eat it raw.

KOHLRABI  Kohlrabi is a member of the cabbage family but resembles a turnip. The edible portion is the enlarged stem just above the ground. It can be grown in spring but is better as a fall crop.

Sow seed in a sunny spot in rich soil ½ inch deep in rows 18 inches apart. Thin seedlings to 4 inches apart. Kohlrabi will need regular watering and several feedings with commercial fertilizers.

Harvest kohlrabi when the swollen stem is about 3 inches in diameter. Cut off tops, peel stem, cut remaining portion into quarters, and cook as you would cabbage or turnips.

LETTUCE  Lettuce is the most popular salad green. There are three main types: heading, leaf, romaine.

Leaf lettuce is one of the fastest maturing garden vegetables, ready to harvest about 6 weeks from seed. The seed sprout in 4 or 5 days. In the spring garden, lettuce does well in full sun, but as the season becomes warmer, find a shadier location to grow lettuce. It grows well interplanted with other vegetables or in the flower garden. It can also be grown in seed flats indoors or on porches and patios.

There are two main types of head lettuce: crisphead (also called iceberg) and butterhead. Crisphead lettuce is the commercial variety found in the grocery store. Butterhead is more tender and does not ship well. Both are excellent for the home gardener. Head lettuce matures in 10 or 11 weeks.

Semiheading lettuce combines the best features of leaf lettuce and the head types.

Romaine lettuce, though less popular than head or leaf lettuce, is actually tastier than either. The plants grow upright to a height of 10 to 12 inches with tightly folded leaves. Romaine is ready for harvest in 9 or 10 weeks.

Lettuce needs well-drained, loose, fertile soil and a partially shaded location. Sow seed 1/4 to 1/2 inch deep in rows 1 1/2 to 2 feet apart. After 2 weeks thin head lettuce to 12 inches between plants, and thin leaf lettuce and romaine to 6 inches between plants. You may transplant thinnings elsewhere.

Lettuce, like cucumbers, is over 95% water, so watering the plants is crucial for proper growth. When rainfall is sparse, water lettuce at least once every 3 or 4 days.

In preparing the seedbed for lettuce mix into the soil 5 pounds of a complete fertilizer per 100 feet of row. At the same time dig in manure or compost. When the plants are 3 weeks old, side-dress with nitrate of soda at the rate of 2 pounds per 100 feet of row. Do not fertilize heading varieties after the heads begin to form.

To keep birds from eating the seedling plants out of your garden, cover the seed rows with chicken wire or hardware cloth. Perhaps the greatest success is assured if you start the seed indoors or in a protected seed flat outdoors, then transplant to the garden when the plants are about 2 weeks old. By using this method, you may give them the proper spacing they will need to grow to maturity.

For winter lettuce, sow seed in partially shaded beds, and transplant to cold frames. Keep the bed well watered, and apply light side-dressings of nitrate of soda every 3 to 4 weeks, except when the plants are heading.

MUSKMELONS   Muskmelons, which include honeydew melons and cantaloupes, grow on sprawling vines and require a fair amount of room.

Prepare seedbed by digging in compost or manure with 5 pounds of complete fertilizer (such as 8-8-8) per 100 feet of row 2 weeks before planting. If a soil test indicates that the soil is too acid, add lime as

Muskmelons (cantaloupes and honeydew melons) need cool, moist, well-drained soil.

directed. Plant 2 to 3 weeks after last expected frost. Muskmelons require 75 to 90 days to reach maturity and cannot tolerate cold.

The hill method of planting is recommended. Plant 5 to 6 seeds in hills 2 feet apart, and thin to one or two plants per hill as they grow. For large plantings space rows of hills 4 to 6 feet apart. Dig a 6-inch deep irrigation trench between the rows of hills or, for small plantings, make trenches around the individual hills. Frequent light waterings are better for melons than excessive soaking. Fill the trench and let it drain; then fill it again. You should do this every 4 or 5 days when there is no rain. Mulching the ground around the vines before they begin to spread will conserve moisture and control weeds. Feed lightly with a commercial fertilizer once a month. One handful per hill scattered in the irrigation trench will suffice.

The fruit is ready to harvest when it separates cleanly from the stem as it is gently lifted. Do not harvest too early, as the melons will not be sweet. Honeydew melons will keep for a month or more stored in a cool, dry place.

MUSTARD GREENS  Mustard greens are grown for their leaves which can be cooked or eaten raw in salads. Mustard greens mature rapidly (25 to 40 days); therefore, a succession of plantings is recommended.

Sow seed ½ inch deep in short rows or patches, and thin seedlings to stand 6 inches apart. Fertilizer recommendations are the same as for turnip greens.

Harvest leaves as they near maturity and are still tender. Keep plants well watered and cut to keep them producing.

OKRA  Okra is a warm-season vegetable and should not be planted until 2 or 3 weeks after the danger of frost has passed and the soil has warmed up. Prepare the seedbed as for other medium-feeding vegetables—5 or 6 pounds of complete fertilizer per 100 feet of row should be dug into the soil with compost or manure about 2 weeks before planting time.

Okra is a warm-weather crop. Harvest the pods when they are about 3 inches long.

Though soaking the seed is not necessary, you may speed germination by soaking the seed for 12 to 24 hours before planting. Plant seed in hills 12 to 18 inches apart. Plant 4 or 5 seeds to a hill, and thin to 2 plants. For row plantings sow seed 3 inches apart, and thin plants to 12 inches apart. Allow 3 feet between rows. Regular watering will be necessary where rainfall is sparse. Make an irrigation trench between rows of hills, or, for small plantings, make a 4-inch deep trench around the individual hills. Scatter a small handful of fertilizer in the irrigation trench for each hill when the pods begin to form.

To keep the plants producing do not allow the pods to mature fully. Harvest them when they are 3 to 4 inches long. Young pods are tastier and more nutritious.

Okra is very susceptible to nematodes. Plant one or two marigolds in each hill of okra, or treat the soil with a commercial nematocide when you prepare the spring seedbed.

ONIONS   The onion family includes green onions, dry onions, garlic, shallots, leeks, and chives.

Onions may be grown from seed, plants, or sets. Sets (small onions grown from seed the previous year and stored in a cool place) and plants are often used for green onions and early dry bulbs.

Onions produce well only in a fertile, finely pulverized soil that is rich in organic matter. Use a balanced fertilizer, 5-10-10, at planting, and side-dress as needed with nitrogen fertilizer to promote good color and growth. Sets should be planted 1 to 1½ inches deep and 1 to 2 inches apart. Seed should be sown ½ inch deep, ¼ inch apart in rows 15 to 18 inches apart, and seedlings thinned to one plant every 2 to 4 inches.

Harvest green onions when they reach edible size. Pull the large ones first to give small ones a chance to develop.

Harvest dry bulb crop after a majority of the tops have broken off. Do not pull them before the outer skin has dried. Then pull bulbs, and leave them on top of the ground to dry and cure for several days.

Onions can be grown from seed or plants. Sow seed in the fall or early spring in the South; set out plants in early spring in the North, or start seed indoors in February to plant outdoors in April.

**LEEKS** Leeks are a substitute for winter green onions and are milder in flavor. Like onions, leeks require a fertile, well-pulverized soil.

Plant seed in beds in later winter, and transplant in early spring, or plant in rows 6 inches apart where they are to grow. To get long, white shanks, plant in trenches 3 to 4 inches deep, and pull soil to them as they grow. By fall enough soil should be pulled around them to make a ridge 4 to 5 inches high. Leeks may be left in the ground during the winter and dug when needed.

Cultivate and fertilize leeks as you do onions.

**SHALLOTS** For fall planting use pieces of bulb (dry sets), and for late winter plantings use green plants. Plant 1 to 1½ inches deep, 2 to 3 inches apart in rows 12 inches apart.

Culture for shallots is much the same as for onions.

**PARSNIPS** Parsnips are excellent for stews or for serving freshly boiled (or broiled), then sliced and fried.

Parsnips are a cool-season root crop, often resembling white carrots or beets, depending on the variety. The soil should be dug deeply as the edible roots will grow 8 to 15 inches into the ground. Pulverize the soil 15 to 18 inches deep, digging in compost or manure and a complete fertilizer at the rate of 6 to 8 pounds per 100 feet of row.

Plant only fresh seed; old seed will not germinate. Plant small pinches of seed about 4 inches apart in the row; then thin the plants to 4 or 5 inches apart. Thinnings may be transplanted elsewhere. Do not handle parsnips when the leaves are wet.

Parsnips are relatively free of pests and diseases.

Side-dress parsnips with complete fertilizer once a month. One or two pounds of complete fertilizer per 100 feet of row will suffice.

Begin to harvest parsnips after the first frost. Cold weather causes the starch to turn to sugar. In most areas of the South, parsnips can be covered with a heavy mulch and left in the ground for winter storage. Dig as needed.

**PEAS, ENGLISH** English peas, also called garden peas, are a cool-season crop and should be among the earliest vegetables planted in the spring. Plant English peas in March or April in the North and as early as January in the middle and lower South. Peas germinate and grow poorly in hot weather, so plant them as early in the season as the ground can be worked. Fertilizer requirements are low; little or no nitrogen is needed for good growth and yield. Taller growing varieties should be staked or trellised, especially where the growing season is long. (The yield of the pole varieties is about twice that for the same length row of shorter varieties.) An excellent trellis can be made by stretching strips of chicken wire (12-inch width) between sturdy posts. About three strips of chicken wire make a trellis 5 to 6 feet tall. Pea vines don't climb by themselves, so you will need to train them on the trellis at first. During the growing season check them to make sure they are clinging to the chicken wire.

Peas do not grow well in acid soil. Since peas and beans have similar soil requirements, it is good to rotate peas with beans. Wherever beans grew well last year, try peas the next year, and vice-versa.

Plant seed about 1 inch deep and 2 inches apart. Rows should be 2 to 3 feet apart for dwarf varieties and 3 to 4 feet apart for taller varieties.

Dwarf varieties mature in 60 to 70 days. Fresh garden peas are delicious raw or cooked. Harvest the pods carefully, taking care not to injure the fragile stems of the plants.

A number of varieties are available, including those that are wilt-resistant and nematode-resistant. Snow peas, with small edible pods, are even hardier than English peas. Chinese food lovers will want to plant some snow peas in the early season garden.

Peas are susceptible to a number of fungus diseases, which can be controlled with a general fungicide such as thiram, Captan, or zineb. Buy seed that has been treated with fungicide if you live in an area of high precipitation. Aphids, mealybugs, and other common insect pests may also attack plants. Most can be controlled with malathion, carbaryl (Sevin), and rotenone, an organic insecticide.

SOUTHERN PEAS, COWPEAS   These include black-eyed peas, crowder peas, field peas, purple-hull peas, and others which, culturally speaking, are beans and are grown as such. Nutritious, tasty, and easy to grow, Southern peas should have a place in any garden. Their unusual tolerance of drought makes them valuable in areas of sparse rainfall. Stagger plantings throughout the first half of the growing season to assure a continuous supply to eat fresh and to preserve.

Southern peas are warm-season vegetables and should not be planted until all danger of frost is passed. Plant seed 2 to 4 inches apart in rows, and space rows 4 feet apart. Plant in hills, if you prefer, with 4 to 6 seeds per hill. Space hills 1 to 2 feet apart. Southern peas may be grown on a trellis where the growing season is long and the vines get straggly. They do not climb by themselves and will need to be tied to their support. Trellising has the advantages of making harvest easier and facilitating weed and pest control.

Make light monthly side-dressings of low-nitrogen fertilizer such as 4-12-12.

PEPPERS   Peppers are ideal for patio containers, hanging baskets, or for filling in empty corners of the flower bed or vegetable garden. They do not require much room, and 10 to 20 plants will be enough for the average family's needs.

Peppers are warm-season vegetables that require a long growing season. Set out plants rather than planting seed to get a head start on the growing season.

Plant peppers in full sunlight 7 to 10 days after the last frost. It is wisest to start seed in a hotbed or in seed flats indoors 3 to 4 weeks before planting time. It may be more practical to buy plants from a nursery or greenhouse, as most gardeners will need so few. Unless the seedbed is very unfertile, it may be best to hold off fertilizing until the first fruits are set; then side-dress with nitrate of soda, ammonium sulfate, or ammonium nitrate. Overfertilizing young pepper plants before the fruit has set can result in bushy growth and few fruits. A rich, sandy loam is best for rapid growth and quality fruit.

For larger plantings set plants 18 to 24 inches apart in rows 3 feet apart. Peppers will need watering at least once a week when there is no rain. Mulch plants with 4 to 6 inches of hay to conserve moisture and control weeds.

Peppers are ready to harvest in 10 or 11 weeks from the time of setting out transplants. Do not allow pods to ripen completely on the plants or they will stop producing. Any pods that are two-thirds grown when the first frost comes may be picked and stored with the rest of the harvest in a cool, dry place.

Sweet peppers freeze well, and excess pods can be chopped or diced and frozen. Frozen pepper is excellent for spaghetti sauces, meat loaves, and other cooking purposes.

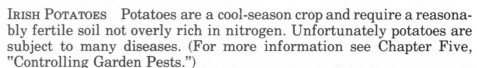

IRISH POTATOES   Potatoes are a cool-season crop and require a reasonably fertile soil not overly rich in nitrogen. Unfortunately potatoes are subject to many diseases. (For more information see Chapter Five, "Controlling Garden Pests.")

Even if light frost nips seedlings, potatoes will not be damaged. Potatoes should be planted in well-prepared ground. Prepare rows 3 to 3½ feet apart, and fertilize with 4-12-12 or 5-10-10 from 7 to 10 days before planting. Grow your potatoes from certified, disease-free seed potatoes cut into chunky pieces 1½ inches square, each chunk containing one or more eyes. Thoroughly water the soil, and place potato pieces, cut side down, 4 inches deep, 12 to 18 inches apart in rows.

If a crust forms before seedlings are up cultivate the topsoil just enough to keep down weeds and grasses. Potato roots need constant moisture; consider mulching to retain moisture.

Dig "new" potatoes when tops begin to flower. Dig mature potatoes when the tops turn brown and die. Take care in harvesting not to damage developing tubers. You might use a garden fork to push gently into the soil and lift up a clump of earth containing potatoes.

Potatoes can be stored in a darkened, well-ventilated place at 50°. (Protection from long exposure to light is necessary to prevent them from becoming green and unfit for table use.)

To ward off insects and diseases, you might try companion planting potatoes and onions; also, don't plant potatoes in soil that has grown tomatoes the previous year, as the soil may be infested with nematodes.

SWEET POTATOES   Sweet potatoes are more nutritious than Irish potatoes but require a lot of space and a warm growing season of 4½ to 5 months.

Sweet potatoes are not easy to grow. Too much fertilization causes bushy vines with small potatoes; insufficient fertilizer can result in no potatoes at all. Excess moisture just before harvesttime causes roots to crack. Sweet potatoes are also susceptible to a number of insects and diseases.

A fertile, sandy soil allows the fruits, which are tubers, to develop without becoming twisted and distorted. Two weeks before planting, fertilize the bed with 5-10-10, 4-12-12, or a comparable fertilizer high in phosphorus and potash and low in nitrogen. On very sandy soils, usually low in potash, an analysis such as 3-9-12 or 3-9-18 is required. Do not use stable manure in the sweet potato bed as this encourages the spread of such diseases as scurf and black rot.

Planting on raised beds is the best method for sweet potatoes; irrigation and harvesting are easier. Purchase slips (rooted cuttings) from the nursery, and set them 10 to 12 inches apart in rows 2 to 3 feet apart. Mulch to conserve moisture and heat in the soil and to control weeds. If a thick mulch (6 to 12 inches) is applied to established plants, sweet potato tubers will form in the mulch also, further facilitating harvesting.

Begin digging sweet potatoes before the first frosts are expected as the vines are easily damaged by the cold. If frost should kill the vines before the potatoes are dug, dig them up immediately. Such potatoes should be used first and not kept in storage.

When digging, avoid cutting roots. Handle sweet potatoes as little as possible, placing them directly in the baskets or containers where they will be stored. Do not put culls or diseased potatoes in with good ones. A root cellar or other cool, dry storage place is required.

PUMPKINS  Pumpkins require a lot of space to grow and are not well suited to a small garden.

Pumpkins may be planted among rows of corn and at the same time as corn. If you are planting in rows sow pumpkin seed 2 to 4 weeks before the last frost, 1 to 2 seeds to the foot in rows 8 to 10 feet apart. Later, thin to one plant every 3 feet. In hill planting plant 2 to 3 seeds to each hill, and space hills 4 to 8 feet apart. Later, thin to one plant per hill. For both methods sow seed 1 inch deep.

Late-planted pumpkins may need watering, then mulching to help them produce before frost.

Once cut from the vine, mature pumpkins may be stored in a cool, dark place (about 50°) for months.

RADISHES  Radishes, the fastest growers in the vegetable garden, mature in 18 to 30 days, depending on the variety. Early spring and mid-fall plantings are best. Radishes grown during hot weather are less desirable. Grown among rows of other root crops, radishes can break up the soil for carrots, beets, or parsnips and be harvested and removed quickly enough so they do not inhibit the slower growers.

Prepare the bed as for other root crops such as carrots, beets, turnips, and the like. A loose, fertile soil is best. Plant seed thinly, about 1 inch apart, and thinning will be unnecessary. Space rows about 12 inches apart.

Water radishes regularly when rainfall is scant. If the radishes seem small, side-dress them lightly with complete fertilizer at the rate of 1 pound per 35 feet of row.

Harvest radishes when sample pickings have reached the desired size and taste. Use them immediately; radishes left in the ground become pithy and lose their taste.

RHUBARB  Rhubarb like a climate that is cool and moist in summer and cold in winter.

Any well-drained, fertile soil in partial shade is suitable for rhubarb. Spade the soil or plow it to a depth of 12 to 16 inches, and mix in rotted

manure, leaf mold, decayed hardwood leaves, sods, or other forms of organic matter. Prepare soil the same as for asparagus. Plant crowns divided from established plants or purchased from a nursery. Plant 3 feet apart in rows 5 feet apart. Before cold weather comes apply a 3- to 4-inch mulch of compost or manure to each row. After each harvest season fertilize each crown with a complete fertilizer.

Rhubarb have to grow for 1 year before they are ready to harvest. To harvest, grab the leaf stalk at the lower end, pull down and to one side until the stalk snaps off cleanly. *Never eat rhubarb leaves. They are poisonous. Use only the stalks.* Rhubarb can be grown in the same soil for up to 8 years. After that dig up the roots, divide, and set them in a new location.

SALSIFY  Salsify, also called oyster plant, is a root vegetable. It is often used in soups and stews or is boiled and sliced for frying. Like other root crops, it is easy to grow and winters well if left in the ground.

Pulverize the soil 10 to 12 inches deep, adding 5 or 6 pounds of complete fertilizer per 100 feet of row. If the soil is very heavy and claylike, add clean builder's sand or vermiculite to improve drainage. Add compost or dried manure to extremely sandy soils to improve moisture retention.

Salsify is a cool-weather vegetable and may run to seed if it is maturing during very warm weather. It is recommended for the fall garden.

Sow seed thinly, and thin young plants to 3 inches apart. Space rows 15 to 18 inches apart. A side-dressing of nitrogen every 6 to 8 weeks will promote good root development.

Salsify matures in 100 to 120 days. Dig roots as they are needed. Where winter temperatures drop below 20° apply a 6- to 8-inch mulch of hay or leaves for protection.

SOYBEANS  Soybeans were being eaten by the ancient Chinese before the Egyptians built the great pyramids, but only recently have soybeans become a food crop for Americans. They are among the most nutritious of vegetables and can be used as a meat substitute in casseroles and for making flour, grits, soy "milk," soy "cheese," and a number of other preparations. Ground, dried soybeans contain up to 50% protein.

Prepare the seedbed in a sunny location on loose, fertile soil. Two weeks before planting, dig in 5 pounds of complete fertilizer per 100 feet of row. Many growers inoculate the soil with nitrogen-fixing bacteria (available at agricultural supply stores) that attach themselves to the roots of the plant—a process called nodulation. Plants that are not inoculated should receive a side-dressing of nitrogen fertilizer every 4 to 6 weeks during their long growing season. One pound of nitrate of soda per 100 feet of row should suffice.

Sow seed thinly (4 inches apart) to avoid having to thin the fragile young plants later. Pulling weeds, which may injure the plants, may be avoided by applying a hay mulch as soon as the plants are 4 or 5 inches tall. Allow 2 feet between rows of early maturing varieties and 2¹/₂ to 3 feet for late varieties.

Most varieties of soybeans are slow growers, requiring from 14 to 18 weeks to reach maturity. Pods will be plump, but the seeds may still be green. This is the point at which soybeans are best for cooking fresh. Allow some plants to ripen a little more to assure a good supply of beans for drying.

To facilitate shelling of beans in the green stage, put the pods in a pan, and cover them with boiling water. Allow them to remain in the water for 5 minutes, then drain them, and allow them to cool. Break the pods across the middle, and squeeze the beans out.

SPINACH  Spinach is a hardy cool-weather plant that withstands winter conditions in the South. In most of the North, spinach is primarily an early-spring and late-fall crop, but in some areas, where summer temperatures are mild, it may be grown continuously from early spring until late fall. It should be emphasized that summer and winter culture of spinach is possible only where moderate temperatures prevail.

Spinach will grow on almost any well-drained, fertile soil where sufficient moisture is available. It is very sensitive to acid soil. If a soil test shows a need, apply lime to the part of the garden used for spinach, regardless of the treatment given the rest of the garden area.

The application of 100 pounds of rotted manure and 3 to 4 pounds of commercial fertilizer to each 100 square feet of land is suitable for spinach in the home garden. Broadcast both manure and fertilizer, and work them in before sowing the seed.

The rows should be 14 to 16 inches apart. Spinach may be drilled by hand in furrows about 1 inch deep and covered with fine earth not more than 1/2 inch deep, or it may be drilled with a seed drill, which distributes the seed more evenly than is ordinarily possible by hand. Thin the plants to 3 or 4 inches apart before they crowd in the row. Harvest by cutting the entire plant.

SQUASH  Squash can be divided into two groups, the summer and the winter varieties. The summer varieties are bush types that are used while young and tender. They are prolific producers and deserve a place in even the small garden. The winter varieties are principally vine types that have hard rinds, making them adaptable for storage. The vine types require considerable space and are not recommended for the small garden.

The cement blocks provide support for these squash plants and create an orderly appearance.

Yellow squash is popular in all regions of the country. Harvest the fruits when they are 6 to 8 inches long.

Squash respond well to manure or other organic matter in the soil. They need liberal doses of a high potassium (potash) fertilizer, such as a 5-10-15, before or at planting and again as a side-dressing in midseason.

Plant bush squash in 3- to 4-foot rows with plants 2 to 3 feet apart in the row. Plant vining types in 6- to 8-foot rows with plants about 4 to 6 feet apart in the row. Sow seed for both types 1 inch deep.

Squash need to be watered frequently but it is important to keep the fruit from rotting as a result of lying on wet ground. To avoid fruit rot make mulch by laying down black plastic and cutting slits in the surface through which to plant and water, or lay a thick, 6-inch mulch of hay or pine straw. (For more information see "Mulching" in Chapter Four, "Routine Garden Care.")

Harvest summer squash while small and tender—before the rind hardens. Leaving fruit on the vines until mature will reduce further setting of young fruit. The winter squash will not store well unless well matured with hard rinds. Store under moderately warm (50°), dry conditions.

Squash are subject to pests and diseases. The cucumber beetle and squash bug, two of the most common pests, can be deterred by companion planting radishes or nasturtiums with squash. (For more information see Chapter Five, "Controlling Garden Pests.")

TOMATOES   Tomatoes need full sun and fertile, well-drained soil. Very little space is required to produce a year's supply of tomatoes for the average family. They may be planted in corners of the garden, among bedding flowers, or in planters.

Sow seed in window boxes or seed flats 5 or 6 weeks before the intended date of transplanting. The seeds germinate best at room temperature—about 70°. Transplant outside only when the danger of frost is past. Plants may be bought ready to set out from nurseries and garden supply stores.

Prepare planting holes 2 weeks in advance. They should be 18 inches wide and 18 inches deep. Mix together 2 parts topsoil to 1 part compost,

Tomatoes are the most commonly grown home garden crop. Select varieties that are resistant to nematodes and wilt diseases.

Buy started plants at a greenhouse or nursery to gain several weeks on the growing season. First, dig a hole deep enough so that half the stem will be below the level of surrounding soil.

Next, remove leaves and stems from the bottom half of the plant.

Set the plant in the hole, firm soil around it, and water well.

peat moss, or dried manure. To this mixture add 1 cup of complete fertilizer.

Space staked plants about 2 to 2½ feet apart in rows 3 to 4 feet apart; unstaked plants require 5 to 6 feet between plants. Set each plant deep in the planting hole, about halfway up the stem, and firm the soil gently over the roots. It is best to set plants on a cloudy day or in late afternoon to avoid severe wilting. Applying a starter solution will help the new plants become established quickly.

Some type of support is recommended. Supported plants are easier to tend and the fruits easier to harvest. Stakes, trellises, teepees, and wire cages all make good supports. To stake follow these steps:

1. Drive stakes (5 to 7 feet long) a foot or more into the ground about 6 inches from the plant.
2. When the first cluster of flowers appears, tie the plants to the stake just above the cluster. Use string, soft twine, or strips of cloth to avoid damaging the tender vines. Do not tie them so tightly that you strangle them.
3. As each new cluster appears, tie the plant to the stake just above the new cluster.

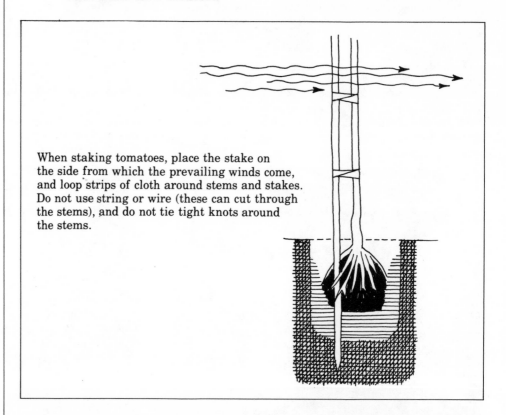

When staking tomatoes, place the stake on the side from which the prevailing winds come, and loop strips of cloth around stems and stakes. Do not use string or wire (these can cut through the stems), and do not tie tight knots around the stems.

If you prune the plants to a single stem, remove all suckers. If you prefer a two-stem method, save the first sucker below the first cluster of flowers (usually the strongest, most vigorous sucker) as the second stem, and remove all the other suckers.

Mulch tomatoes to conserve moisture. Adequate moisture is crucial for the development of young fruits. Plants should be watered deeply every 4 to 6 days when rainfall is scant.

After the fruit has set side-dress every 3 to 4 weeks with nitrogen fertilizer at the rate of 1 pound per 100 feet of row. Many preparations are available commercially under the name "tomato food." Wait until fruit has set before applying fertilizer regularly. The two most frequent

Tomatoes are most productive when staked or grown on other support. Here, a circular wire cage is placed over each tomato plant.

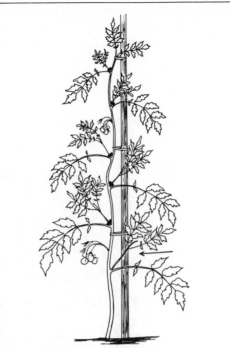

Small shoots that grow in the crotches formed by branches and stems are called suckers, because they sap energy from fruit production. Remove suckers at the point of origin, and discard them or plant them in the ground to obtain additional plants. Plant them deep enough that the lower half of the stem is below soil level.

reasons for blossom drop are inadequate sun exposure and too much nitrogen fertilizer applied too soon.

Constant vigilance is required to keep tomatoes free of insects and diseases. Plant only nematode-resistant varieties. (For more information see Chapter Five, "Controlling Garden Pests.") Avoid smoking tobacco around tomato plants as packaged tobacco products may contain tobacco mosaic disease. Placing paper cups or other collar-type protectors around the base of the tomato plant helps reduce infestation by cutworms.

A popular method of supporting tomatoes is called the Japanese tomato ring. For this you will need the following supplies: a piece of wire fence 5 feet high and 15 feet long, 2 pounds of complete fertilizer, two wheelbarrow loads of good soil, a small bottle of nematocide. To make the ring follow these steps:

1. Choose a sunny location. Pulverize the soil to a depth of 6 inches, and add the nematocide solution according to label directions.
2. Form the length of wire into a cylinder by joining and attaching the ends. Place this in the center of the broken ground.
3. Place a 6-inch layer of mulch in the bottom of the wire cage. Add a layer of soil, another layer of mulch, and a second layer of soil. Mix two handfuls of fertilizer with the top layer of soil and treat the mixture with nematocide. Pull material away from the center toward the edges, making the pile dish-shaped so that it will hold water.

4. After 1 week, set 3 or 4 tomato plants at equal intervals around the outside of the cage, and apply a starter solution. (For more information, see "Making and using starter solutions" in Chapter Two, "Planting the Garden.") As young plants grow, they will develop roots in the soil and in the mulch.
5. Tie the plants to the wire as they grow. When the fruits are well set and growing, add 5 pounds of nitrogen fertilizer to the mixture in the cage, and water it in.

Japanese tomato ring makes the most of a large compost heap by using the wire cage as support for the plants. The ring is most practical in cool regions where plants may grow only 3 or 4 feet high.

TURNIPS AND RUTABAGAS   Turnips and rutabagas are closely related root crops. The only significant difference between the two is the longer maturation period required for rutabaga. Rutabagas generally store better than turnips. Both are rich in vitamin A, and their leaves are rich in vitamins A and C.

Turnips and rutabagas are cool-season crops and may be planted as soon as the ground is warm enough to work.

Prepare seedbed as for beets, carrots, and other root crops. They require a deep, finely pulverized soil that allows the roots room to grow. Sow seed thinly enough so that the 2- to 3-inch plants may be thinned to 2 inches apart. Rows should be about 18 inches apart. Make successive plantings every 3 or 4 weeks.

Turnips and rutabagas appreciate regular watering. A feeding of nitrogen fertilizer once a month at the rate of 1 pound per 100 feet of row will speed the roots to maturity. They are fast growers and will be ready to harvest in 6 to 8 weeks. Do not store turnips with other fruits and vegetables as the turnip odor will taint them. Rutabagas may be left in the ground (apply protective mulch where winter temperatures stay below 20°), but turnips become woody if they are left more than a few weeks.

WATERMELONS  Watermelons are grown much like cantaloupes, but they need even more room to grow. Knowing when to harvest is trickier. "Thumping" the melon is a common method of determining ripeness. Strike the melon near the center with the heel of your hand; an unripe melon gives a ringing sound, whereas a ripe melon gives a dull thud.

Another method is to watch the tendril (often referred to as the "curly pig's tail") where the melon attaches to the vine. With many varieties, the pig's tail shrivels and turns brown at maturity or a few days before. A curled, brown-tailed melon should be thumped to determine precise time of maturity. Ripe melons lose their smooth finish and become dull in appearance.

Place growing melons on blocks of wood or tin cans to increase sun exposure and sweetness of the fruit.

# Herb Gardens

Herbs have been prized for centuries for their fragrance, taste, and medicinal properties. But there is nothing mysterious or difficult about growing them. Herbs are remarkably durable plants. They have an affinity for sun and will tolerate almost any soil so long as it is well drained.

Your herb garden can be anything from a yard-square patch near the kitchen door to a formal decorative garden 200 feet square. Herbs also are excellent container plants and do well in pots, boxes, planters, and raised beds. Many, such as parsley, make attractive border plants for vegetable gardens and flower beds. Others, including rosemary and spearmint, are effective controls for insects and worms when used as companion plants with vegetables. (For more information see "Companion planting" in Chapter Nine, "Organic Vegetable Gardening.")

This two-year-old thyme was planted in a pot and left outdoors all winter in Atlanta.

## Herb Garden Design

In choosing plants for an herb garden consider those that are purely ornamental and those that you will use in cooking. Spacing and locating herbs in the bed are particularly important in more formal gardens. No geometrically correct plan is possible unless particular heights and habits of plants are known. The following layout is one you might try.

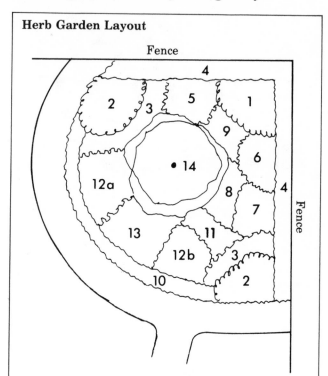

**Herb Garden Layout**

A corner of a fence is an excellent location for an herb garden, especially if a small ornamental tree such as a dogwood or redbud can be employed to give the herb garden focus and filtered shade. 1. Rosemary, 2. Sage, 3. Chives, 4. Dill, 5. Spearmint, 6. Peppermint, 7. Apple mint, 8. Winter savory, 9. Oregano, 10. Parsley, 11. Sweet marjoram, 12. Basil (a) green, (b) purple, 13. Thyme, and 14. Dogwood or small tree.

### GROWING HERBS

Because good drainage is essential for growing herbs successfully, consider using containers or raised beds if your soil drains poorly. Sage, rosemary, thyme, parsley, and mint grow well in raised beds.

Some herbs such as the following may be

started from seed: dill, parsley, sweet marjoram, chives, sweet basil, summer and winter savory. Others should be started from crown divisions or rooted cuttings: oregano, rosemary, sage, tarragon, and thyme.

## Drying Herbs

Herbs should be gathered just when buds open into full flower. This is the point at which they are the most flavorful and fragrant. Harvest herbs on a dry morning after the dew is gone and before the sun is high. Cut perennials about two-thirds of the way down the stalk; cut annuals back to 3 to 4 inches high. This will stimulate second growth. Rinse leaves to remove any loose dirt, but do not soak.

A good drying method is to lay strips of herbs on window screens; take care to keep herbs separate. Cover them with cheesecloth, and lay them propped on blocks or chairs in the attic. (Any dark, ventilated room will do.) When sufficiently dry, herbs will be crisp.

Store herbs in airtight containers to prevent loss of essential oils and delicate flavor.

In this herb garden are (back row) dill, mint, parsley; (front) chives, sage, thyme.

## Popular Culinary Herbs

Culinary herbs are garden plants grown for seasoning food and beverages. (Where plants are started from seed, plant them ½ inch deep.) The following is a list of popular culinary herbs.

ANISE (Pimpinella anisum)   1½-foot annual. Sow seed in early spring. Requires light, fertile, sandy loam, well drained. Use leaves in salads and as garnish; use licorice-flavored seed in pastries, candies, beverages.

BASIL (Ocimum basilicum)   2-foot annual. Sow seed or transplant seedlings in spring in sun or partial shade. Remove seed stalks as they mature. Use leaves with tomatoes, cucumbers, green salads, in all egg dishes, in poultry stuffings.

BORAGE (Borago officinalis)   1- to 3-foot annual. Sow seed in late fall or early spring in sunny, well-drained moist soil. Keep plant cut back. Leaves give cucumber taste to salads; flowers may be candied by cutting them fresh, dipping them in egg whites then sugar, and drying them.

CARAWAY (Carum carvi)  2-foot biennial. Plant in spring or fall. Grows in wide range of soil conditions. Locate away from site likely to receive heavy rain and severe winds. Use leaves to garnish, flavor salads; use seed in potato salad, cottage or cream cheese, bread, cakes, pastries.

CHERVIL (Anthriscus cerefolium)  2-foot annual. Sow seed in early spring or late summer in moist, well-drained soil in partial shade. Use leaves in salads, soups, with oysters, and as garnish.

CHIVES (Allium schoenoprasum)  6-inch perennial. Start from seed or by dividing clumps of bulbs. Plant in spring or fall in sun or partial shade. Need periodic dividing. Use chopped leaves in soups, salads, stews, sour cream, dips, dressings.

CORIANDER (Coriandrum sativum)  2½-foot annual. Sow seed spring or fall in sunny spot. Thrives on rich garden loam. Use seed in candies, sauces, French dressing, soups, beverages.

DILL (Anethum graveolens)  2½-foot annual. Sow in spring or fall in full sun. Grows on nearly all soil types. Harvest mature seedheads before they shed. Do not transplant. Use dried seed in pickling cucumbers, and for preparing meats, fish, chicken, vegetables.

HOREHOUND (Marrubium vulgare)  Perennial. Sow seed in early spring; may be transplanted from cold frame. Grows in any soil. Use in horehound candy.

LOVAGE (Levisticum officinale)  Perennial. Plant seed in fall, or sow in early spring in hotbed, greenhouse, or in a well-prepared, sheltered seedbed in the garden. Locate in partial shade in fertile, deep moist soil. Cover with old burlap, and sprinkle occasionally. Remove cover when first seedlings appear. Use celery-tasting leaves in soups, stews, potato salad; seed, whole or ground, in meat pies, salads, candies.

SWEET MARJORAM (Majorana hortensis)  1-foot perennial. Start from seed or from cutting or crown divisions in fall or spring in full sun. Makes good border plant. Use leaves in mashed potatoes, salads, poultry seasonings, meat, casseroles, gravies, soups, eggs.

MINT (peppermint, spearmint, apple mint, pineapple mint)  2-foot perennial. Grow from seed, from divisions of root stock, or from cuttings in moist soil. Use leaves to flavor lamb, peas, soups, tea, fruit drinks.

ORECANO (Origanum vulgare) 2-foot perennial. Does best started from rooted cuttings or crown divisions, but may be started from seed. Keep in bounds by edging and clipping. Use leaves in Spanish, Mexican, and Italian dishes.

PARSLEY (Petroselinum crispum) 10-inch biennial. Sow in full sun or partial shade. Easily started from seed or transplants. Needs fertile soil with good moisture-holding ability. Excellent border plant. Use leaves in sauces, meat loaves, soups, casseroles, cocktails, sandwiches, and garnishes.

ROSEMARY (Rosmarinus officinalis) 3-foot perennial. Plant in spring in full sun in poor but well-drained soil. Does best started from rooted cuttings, but can be started from seed. Needs periodic clipping to check growth. Use leaves sparingly in soups, poultry, lamb, stews, and sauces.

SAGE (Salvia officinalis) 2-foot perennial. Plant in spring or fall in sun or partial shade. May be started from seed but, because of seedling variation, does best started from stem cuttings or crown divisions. Clip plant to check growth. Use leaves sparingly in soups, sauces, stews, cream or cottage cheese, and fowl stuffings.

SUMMER SAVORY (Satureia hortensis) 1½-foot annual. Sow seed or transplant in full sun. Control by clipping. Plant tends to fall over unless soil is mounded around base. Use leaves in green beans, soups, stuffings, veal and poultry sauces, egg dishes, and salads.

WINTER SAVORY (Satureia montana) 1½-foot perennial. Easily started from seed, rooted cuttings, or crown divisions. Use leaves as accent to chicken and turkey stuffings, sausage, and some egg dishes.

TARRAGON (Artemisia dracunculus) 2- to 3-foot perennial. Can be grown only from cuttings or crown divisions. Plant in full sun or light shade in poor soil. Specify French tarragon (dracunculus) because Russian tarragon is a different plant. Trim during growing season to keep new, tender shoots coming on. Leaves can be the leading accent in green salads, salad dressings, vinegars, fish sauces, tartar sauces, and some egg dishes.

THYME (Thymus vulgaris) 1-foot perennial. May be started from seed but does best started from root cuttings or divisions. Plant in spring or fall in sun or partial shade and poor, dry soil. Use fresh leaves in salads; dried leaves in meat dishes, gravies, and dressings.

# Growing Vegetables in Containers

Container gardening is at least as old as the hanging gardens of Biblical Babylon, and probably older. Since man has moved into cities, he has endeavored to bring plants with him. Today container-grown plants range from woodland mosses in a terrarium to mature banana trees in a greenhouse.

Growing vegetables in containers is not difficult if you can provide a sunny location for your plants and give them the daily attention they will require. Decks, patios, walkways, and other areas with limited space make excellent locations for container vegetable gardens. In fact, the more limited the area, the more effective the plants become as ornamentals. Ornamental value and interest will have to be the primary motives for raising a container vegetable garden, and, of course, a few delicious vegetables. But don't plan on filling your freezer.

## Vegetables for Container Culture

Not all vegetables lend themselves well to container gardening. Corn is impractical (successful pollination requires a substantial planting) as are pumpkins and watermelons. But eggplant, peppers, cherry tomatoes, and many herbs perform quite well in the right container in the right place.

In general, select plants of a compact habit for container culture. This is not to eliminate tall plants such as okra which is a superb container plant planted alone in a pot or massed in a large tub.

Big enough for one large-type tomato, this wooden basket has three cherry-type plants.

In a sunny spot, tomatoes in containers will bear fruit for a long period of time.

## Containers

Your selection of plants will depend largely on the containers you plan to use. The most commonly available containers are planters and large pots. These are suitable for a number of vegetable plants. The most versatile container, however, is a trough-style planter. Nearly anything that is grown as a row crop in the garden will thrive in such a container. A window box is excellent for English peas, bush beans, peppers, eggplant, or ornamental kale.

Of limited use but unlimited attractiveness is the hanging container. Not many vegetable plants are well suited to hanging baskets, but climbing vines such as pole beans and black-eyed peas can be grown in large containers and trained to cascade. English peas are a good choice for a simple hanging basket. Plant a few nasturtiums or sweetpeas in the basket with them.

Tomatoes, pole beans, and other climbers can be grown in troughs or tubs if support is provided. Trellises are the most attractive means of support and can be fashioned to train plants to appealing forms.

A miniature variety of cucumber will do quite well in a plastic hanging basket.

This growing ring was assembled on a concrete drive; cucumbers are planted in it.

*Trough or Window Box*

| | |
|---|---|
| Bush beans | Lettuce |
| English peas | Onions |
| Cabbage | Garlic |
| Collards | Herbs |
| Mustard | Turnips |
| Celery | Carrots |
| Broccoli | Beets |
| Cauliflower | Brussels sprouts |
| Eggplant | Turnip greens |
| Kohlrabi | |

*Trough with trellis*

| | |
|---|---|
| Pole beans | Black-eyed peas |
| Tomatoes | Pinto beans |

*Pot*

| | |
|---|---|
| Okra | Eggplant |
| Tomato | Cabbage |
| Chard | Lettuce (leaf) |
| Herbs | Onions |
| Peppers | Garlic |
| Brussels sprouts | |

*Hanging basket*

| | |
|---|---|
| English peas, snow peas | Cherry tomato |
| Pickling cucumber | Herbs |
| Sweet potato | |

*Tub*
Squash
Tomatoes
Combinations
        Beets

Okra
Asparagus
Carrots

## Locating the Container Garden

Porches, decks, patios, balconies, steps, and other prominent areas are good locations for container plants. Pruning considerations in locating plants include light and exposure to heavy rain or drying winds. Although vegetable plants in the open ground prefer full sun, container-grown plants should receive filtered sun. In full sun the soil can dry quickly leaving plants susceptible to sunscorch. Full sun for part of the day, especially in the morning, will benefit most container-grown vegetables, but do not expose them to midday sun during the summer.

## Soil for Container Gardens

Most vegetables will grow well in a mixture of equal parts garden loam, sand (or perlite), and peat moss. Finely ground compost, leaf mold, and rotted sawdust are excellent alternatives to peat moss. Such a mixture is moisture

Vegetables are growing in redwood planters set on a 5- × 10-foot apartment balcony.

## CULTURAL REQUIREMENTS OF CONTAINER-GROWN VEGETABLES

| Plant | Light | When to plant | Days from seed to harvest | Space between plants (inches) | Planting depth (inches) | When to harvest |
|-------|-------|---------------|---------------------------|-------------------------------|-------------------------|-----------------|
| Beets | Tolerate partial shade | 2 to 4 weeks before frost-free date | 50 to 60 | 2 to 3 | 1/2 | When 1 to 2 inches in diameter |
| | | *Comment: Thin plants when 6 to 8 inches high; use thinnings for greens.* | | | | |
| Cabbage | Tolerates partial shade | Set out plants 4 to 6 weeks before frost-free date | 65 to 120, depending on variety | 12 to 18 | 1/2 (for seed); bury roots of plants | When head is hard and rounded |
| | | *Comment: Can also be set out for a fall crop.* | | | | |
| Carrots | Tolerate partial shade | 2 to 4 weeks before frost-free date | 65 to 80 | 2 to 3 | 1/2 | For small carrots, when 1/2 to 1 inch in diameter |
| | | *Comment: To get several harvests, make plantings at 3-week intervals until 3 months before fall freezing date.* | | | | |
| Chives | Grow in partial shade, as in kitchen window | Set out plants 4 to 6 weeks before frost-free date (can also be started from seed) | 60 to 70 | 2 to 3 (in clusters) | 1/2 | Clip as needed for salads, toppings |
| | | *Comment: Bulbs should be divided occasionally, so that they do not get too thick.* | | | | |

| Plant | Light | When to plant | Days from seed to harvest | Space between plants (inches) | Planting depth (inches) | When to harvest |
|---|---|---|---|---|---|---|
| Cucumbers | Require full sunlight | Set out plants 1 week after frost-free date | 70 to 80 | 18 | ½ (for seed); bury roots of plants | For best yield, pick before hard seeds form |

*Comment: Need hot weather. Use container of at least 5-gallon size. Start seeds in pots or berry boxes about 3 weeks before time to set out. During early growth, cover with a paper or plastic tent during cool nights.*

| | | | | | | |
|---|---|---|---|---|---|---|
| Eggplant | Needs full sunlight | Set out plants on frost-free date; they require warm soil | 100 to 140 | One plant to a 3-gallon container | ½ (for seed); bury roots of plants | When fruits are mature |

*Comment: Hard to grow in northern parts of U.S. because of high heat requirement and long growing season. Cover the plants during cool periods. You might want to try the new dwarf varieties. Start seeds indoors 8 to 9 weeks before transplanting time.*

| | | | | | | |
|---|---|---|---|---|---|---|
| Kale | Tolerates partial shade | 6 to 8 weeks before first fall freeze | 55 to 70 | 6 | ½ | When tall enough for greens; cut whole plants or take larger leaves |

*Comment: Very winter hardy. Plant also in early fall for winter crops.*

| | | | | | | |
|---|---|---|---|---|---|---|
| Leek | Tolerates partial shade | 4 to 6 weeks before frost-free date | 130 | 2 to 3 | ½ | When 1 inch in diameter and white part is 5 to 6 inches long |

*Comment: Leek is a decorative and winter-hardy plant.*

| | | | | | | |
|---|---|---|---|---|---|---|
| Leaf lettuce | Tolerates partial shade | 4 to 6 weeks before frost-free date and 6 to 8 weeks before first fall freeze | 30 to 35 | 4 to 6 | ¼ | Cut leaves when large enough to use |

*Comment: Lettuce is a cool-weather crop. It can be started inside early and set out even before frosts end. Plants will tolerate temperatures as low as 28° F. You can make several later plantings for summer lettuce unless hot weather hinders growth.*

| | | | | | | |
|---|---|---|---|---|---|---|
| Mustard greens | Tolerate partial shade | 2 to 4 weeks before frost-free date until 6 to 8 weeks before first fall freeze | 35 to 40 | 4 to 5 | ¼ | When large enough to make greens |

*Comment: Can be grown throughout the summer. You can make plantings at 10-day intervals for successive crops.*

| | | | | | | |
|---|---|---|---|---|---|---|
| Onions | Green onions grow in partial shade; mature bulbs need full sun | Plant bulb sets 4 to 6 weeks before frost-free date | 100 to 120 (less time for green onions) | 2 to 3 | 1 to 1½ | When large enough for green onions (8 to 10 inches tall); after they dry out they are usable as cooking onions |

*Comment: Onions like lots of moisture.*

| Plant | Light | When to plant | Days from seed to harvest | Space between plants (inches) | Planting depth (inches) | When to harvest |
|---|---|---|---|---|---|---|
| Parsley | Does well in partial shade; will grow on kitchen windowsills | Set out plants 4 to 6 weeks before frost-free date | 85 | 6 to 8 | 1/4 | Clip for garnish |

*Comment: Sensitive to heat. Parsley seeds germinate slowly; soak them in water overnight before planting. Cover container for a few days after planting to keep soil moist. Start indoors if possible.*

| Plant | Light | When to plant | Days from seed to harvest | Space between plants (inches) | Planting depth (inches) | When to harvest |
|---|---|---|---|---|---|---|
| Peppers | Require full sunlight | Set out plants 1 week after frost-free date | 110 to 120 | 14 to 18 | 1/2 (for seed); bury roots of plants | When peppers are 2 to 3 inches in diameter (depends on variety) |

*Comment: Require hot weather. If you start your own seeds indoors, plant 5 or 6 weeks before transplanting time. Allow one plant per 1-gallon container.*

| Plant | Light | When to plant | Days from seed to harvest | Space between plants (inches) | Planting depth (inches) | When to harvest |
|---|---|---|---|---|---|---|
| Radishes (mild) | Do well in partial shade | 2 to 4 weeks before frost-free date | 25 to 35 | 1 | 1/2 | When 1/2 to 1 inch in diameter |

*Comment: Cannot withstand heat. The faster they grow, the better the quality. Be sure they get fertilizer at seeding time. Radishes are at their best for only a few days, so you may wish to make several plantings at 1-week intervals. You may also want to try the hotter, large, winter radishes, which need 75 days or more growing time and are planted to mature just before fall frost.*

| Plant | Light | When to plant | Days from seed to harvest | Space between plants (inches) | Planting depth (inches) | When to harvest |
|---|---|---|---|---|---|---|
| Summer squash | Does best in full sunlight | On frost-free date | 50 to 60 | One plant per 5-gallon container | 1 to 2 | Depends on variety; see your seed package |

*Comment: Plant the bush types of this vegetable.*

| Plant | Light | When to plant | Days from seed to harvest | Space between plants (inches) | Planting depth (inches) | When to harvest |
|---|---|---|---|---|---|---|
| Swiss chard | Tolerates partial shade | 2 to 4 weeks before frost-free date | 30 to 40 | 4 to 5 | 1/2 | When leaves are 3 inches or more in length |

*Comment: Only one planting is necessary; new leaves replace the harvested leaves. Outer leaves may be harvested without injuring the plant. Each seed cluster contains several seeds.*

| Plant | Light | When to plant | Days from seed to harvest | Space between plants (inches) | Planting depth (inches) | When to harvest |
|---|---|---|---|---|---|---|
| Tomatoes | Require full sunlight | Transplant on frost-free date (start seeds 5 to 7 weeks before transplanting) | 55 to 100 | One plant per 1- to 3-gallon container | 1/2 (for seed); bury roots of plants | When tomatoes turn pink or almost red |

*Comment: Dwarf tomatoes offer a large return for a small space. They need warm weather. The Tiny Tim and other dwarf varieties do well in containers.*

| Plant | Light | When to plant | Days from seed to harvest | Space between plants (inches) | Planting depth (inches) | When to harvest |
|---|---|---|---|---|---|---|
| Turnips | Tolerate partial shade | 4 to 6 weeks before frost-free date and 6 to 8 weeks before first fall freeze | 30 to 80 (30 days for greens) | 3 to 4, when harvesting for greens | 1/2 | Thin when large enough to make greens; leave others to mature (2 inches or more in diameter) |

United States Department of Agriculture

New Zealand spinach and leaf lettuce grow well in only a few hours of daily sunlight.

When planting in a container, fill the bottom of the container with gravel or broken crockery to assure good drainage.

retentive and, at the same time, permits excess moisture to drain. You may also buy packaged potting soil at garden supply centers. The greatest advantage of packaged mixes is that the soil has been sterilized. To sterilize your own soil mix, place soil on cookie sheets and bake in the oven at 200° for 1 hour. Sterilization kills nematodes (destructive soil organisms), fungi, and weed seed.

Containers for plants must have drainage holes either in the bottom or in the sides near

Next, fill the container with soil and/or compost, and plant seeds or plants.

the base. Fill the bottom of the container with 1 inch of gravel or charcoal, and add 1 inch of sphagnum moss or other organic matter on top of the gravel. Fill to within 1 inch of the top of the container with soil mix. Sow seed at the depth recommended on the seed packet, and water the planted container thoroughly.

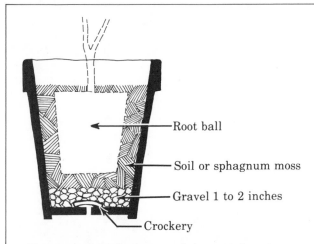

— Root ball

— Soil or sphagnum moss

— Gravel 1 to 2 inches

— Crockery

Place gravel in the bottom of the container to provide good drainage. Dig plants out of the garden with soil attached to roots (root ball), and pot them; or sow seed directly in pots or flats.

*Growing Vegetables in Containers* 89

Boxes and tubs make good containers for vegetable gardening. From left to right; tomatoes, collards, lettuce (fluffy leaves), onions (slender, grasslike leaves), English peas, and more tomatoes.

### Watering the Container Garden

Water will evaporate from containers more quickly on hot, sunny days than on cloudy days. Check plants daily, and learn to gauge watering needs by the appearance of the plants and by feeling the soil. A watering can is best for irrigating container gardens; a hose may wash soil away from roots. On hot, dry days mist the foliage with a fine spray from the garden hose.

Moisture will evaporate from hanging containers faster than containers on the ground. Check hanging baskets daily to see if they need water.

### Fertilizing Container-Grown Plants

Liquid concentrates, sold as house plant fertilizer, are excellent for use on container-grown vegetables. Other suitable fertilizers include cottonseed meal and dehydrated manures. Liquid fertilizers are convenient and easy to apply. You can make your own liquid if you purchase water-soluble fertilizer. Be sure to specify to the retailer that you intend to make such a liquid fertilizer, then mix the solution according to label directions. Cottonseed meal and manure, although they are not water-soluble, can release small quantities of plant nutrients over an extended period. Both also minimize the danger of fertilizer burn.

Apply liquid fertilizer in mild solution once a week. Apply cottonseed meal and manure once a month. For most plants, 1 teaspoon per plant per month will suffice.

Plastic containers holding peppers and tomatoes were added to three sides of cart.

When fully planted, the cart looks cumbersome to move, but large wheels make for easy rolling.

## Insect and Disease Control

All the insects that attack garden vegetables can also attack container vegetables. Control is easier in the container garden because there are fewer plants and because quarantine is possible when a plant is infested.

Hand picking is the best method of insect control in a container garden, unless you are squeamish. A good spraying with a garden or sink hose or a sponge bath will remove insects. Use two sponges, and wipe both the under and top surfaces of leaves at the same time. Wipe stems too.

Several insecticides are also useful (see Chapter Five, "Controlling Pests"). Rotenone, Sevin, and malathion will control insect populations in a container vegetable garden.

Fungus diseases and nematodes can be averted by buying sterilized potting soil or by sterilizing the soil for small containers yourself.

## Growing Plants Without Soil

Growing plants in water is called hydroponics, water culture, tank farming, chemical gardening, and "soil-less" culture. In recent years the term hydroponics has been more generally used.

Growing plants by such methods is generally the same as when using soil, except that the necessary plant nutrients are dissolved in

Oregano, lemon balm, parsley, chives, and marjoram fill this large hanging basket.

Herbs growing in these strawberry jars include chives, oregano, parsley, marjoram, lovage, rosemary, tarragon, and lemon balm.

water rather than in the soil. This is not always as simple as it may sound, since at least 11 plant nutrients must be supplied in proper balance. Three of these (nitrogen, phosphorus, and potassium) are called major elements because plants need more of them. Three of the nutrients are called secondary elements (calcium, magnesium, and sulfur). The remainder of the nutrients are called trace minerals (iron, manganese, boron, copper, and zinc). In some cases molybdenum in trace amounts may need to be added.

Because of widespread interest in hydroponics as a hobby, several "package mixtures" are now available. These mixtures contain all the plant nutrients needed and come either as soluble powders or as liquid concentrates to be diluted with water. These commercial mixtures make hydroponic culture of plants much simpler.

Growing vegetables and flowers by hydroponics is neither practical nor economical, but it is a satisfying hobby for many people. Here are four methods for growing plants without soil: water culture, peat-lite mix culture, sand culture, and gravel culture.

## WATER CULTURE

For this method, plants must first be sprouted or rooted in sand or soil, then transferred to the nutrient solution. Plants are supported by $1/4$-inch mesh screening, cloth, or plywood with drilled holes. It is also good to place on top of this support an inch or two of excelsior, shavings, or moss. The support is lowered into position so that the roots are submerged in the nutrient solution. At first the screen should be at water level, but as plants grow larger, 2 inches of air space should be allowed between the screen and the surface of the solution. Tanks for the solution may be quart jars, large-mouthed jugs, earthenware or glass crocks, or waterproof tanks. Such tanks may be built of concrete, wood, or metal and coated with a pure grade of asphalt (not tar).

The biggest problem with water culture is aerating the water. Water does not retain enough free oxygen to supply plant roots, especially to large plants. Therefore, a device to aerate water, such as the one used for bubbling air into small fish aquariums, is needed. Also, use of nutrients by the plant changes the concentration in the water, so the nutrient solution should be replaced or changed fairly often. Between changings replace the solution as it is used by the plant so that the proper water level can be maintained.

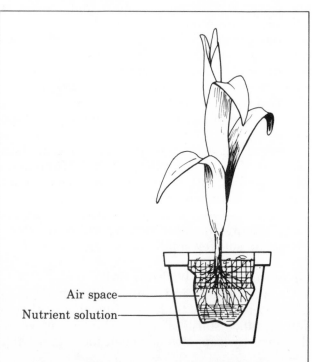

Air space

Nutrient solution

Crock or jar holds nutrient solution. The plant is supported by an excelsior pad. Roots grow through pad and air space into the nutrient solution.

## ARTIFICIAL SOIL MIXES

Several basic artificial soil mixes, referred to as peat-lite mixes, have been developed. These artificial soils offer the grower several advantages: they have a known fertility value; they are sterile and do not require sterilization to control insects, weeds, and nematodes, provided care is taken in mixing and handling; they

## SAND CULTURE

With this method, plants are grown in such materials as clean sand, sawdust, wood shavings, cinders, brick screenings, perlite, vermiculite, peat moss, or haydite. Containers can be 5-gallon cans, flowerpots, or raised benches and should have holes in their bottoms to allow drainage.

|  | For 1 cubic yard | For 2 bushels |
|---|---|---|
| Shredded sphagnum peat moss | 11 bushels | 1 bushel |
| Horticultural vermiculite #2, 3, or 4 | 11 bushels | 1 bushel |
| Ground limestone | 5 pounds | 10 T[1] |
| Superphosphate, 20%, powdered | 2 pounds | 5 T[1] |
| 5-10-5 fertilizer | 6 pounds | 15 T[1] |
| Borax (11% B) | 10 grams (1 level tablespoon) | Do not add |
| Iron (Chelated such as NaFe, 138, or 330) | 25 grams (2 level tablespoons) | 1 level teaspoon |
| Nonionic surfactant[2] | 2 ounces | 1 level teaspoon |

[1]Level tablespoon amounts.
[2]Mixed with 10 to 20 gallons of water/cubic yard of mix; 1 gallon for 2-bushel amount.

have a high moisture-holding capacity, yet drain well.

These are available as commercial products under brand names such as Jiffy-Mix, Kys-Mix, and Peat-Lite Mix, and can be purchased from garden centers and nursery supply dealers. Or you can mix your own using the above formulae.

Thorough mixing of the components is essential; they should be turned several times to be sure they are well mixed. Mixing and storing should be done under sanitary conditions to keep mix sterile. All tools, containers, and mixing areas should be washed with a disinfectant or steam-sterilized to help prevent contamination.

If the peat moss is very dry, a gallon of warm water per 2 bushels of medium-grade moss will aid in keeping the dust down and permit easier wetting and handling. (If possible, add water to peat moss several hours before mixing with other ingredients so it will be uniformly damp.)

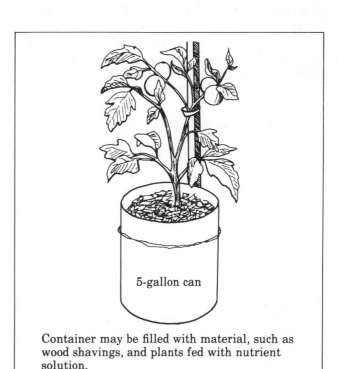

5-gallon can

Container may be filled with material, such as wood shavings, and plants fed with nutrient solution.

The material is moistened with the nutrient solution two or three times a week as needed to keep it moist. Add enough solution each time to set the material all the way to the bottom of the container or bed. Every few weeks water thoroughly with plain water to leach any excess plant nutrient salts that may accumulate and slow down plant growth.

Organic materials, such as sawdust and shavings, will use up part of the nutrients in the process of decay and will shrink or settle somewhat in 3 or 4 months. This does not usually cause trouble, however. At the end of the crop's growing season, the shrunken material makes an excellent mulch for flowers and shrubs.

### GRAVEL CULTURE

This is sometimes called the subirrigation method. Plants are set in a coarse, inorganic medium such as washed river gravel. Containers can be anything from flowerpots to shallow, waterproof beds made of concrete, wood, or metal. Metal containers should be treated to prevent corrosion and the possibility of toxic chemical by-products.

Concrete fiber glass beds are most commonly used by commercial hydroponic growers and gardeners. The nutrient solution flows or is pumped into the bed until it is within an inch or so of surface of the gravel. It is then pumped out or allowed to flow out by gravity into a reservoir or tank for reuse. Beds are flooded from one to five times a day, depending on seasonal temperature, size of plants, and fineness of the gravel. The bed must be flooded often enough to prevent plants from wilting. A simple home subirrigation unit is shown in the sketch.

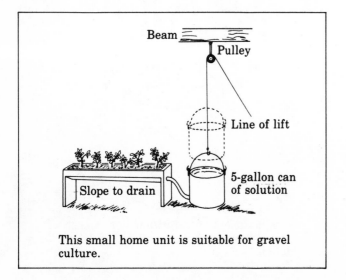

This small home unit is suitable for gravel culture.

A small, windowsill unit can be made of two flowerpots. One should be two sizes larger than the other, such as a 5- and a 7-inch pot, and be of the same shape. The larger one must be made of waterproof material such as plastic, ceramic, or glass. The smaller one, which contains the plant, should be a porous clay pot, filled with coarse sand or fine gravel. Using these two pots, construction is as follows:

- Prepare a collar made of plywood or a similar material with a hole large enough to accommodate the smaller pot. The collar rests on top of the larger pot.
- Pour the nutrient solution into the larger pot until the solution is level with the bottom of the smaller clay pot when sitting in place in the collar.
- Remove the smaller pot from the collar once or twice each day, and lower it into the larger pot. The solution will rise to the top of the gravel through the hole in the bottom.
- Then lift out the smaller pot, place it back in the collar, and allow it to drain.

This method can be used for almost any small plant that is suited to pot culture.

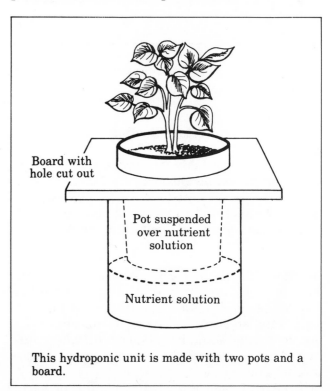

Board with hole cut out

Pot suspended over nutrient solution

Nutrient solution

This hydroponic unit is made with two pots and a board.

### MAKING NUTRIENT SOLUTIONS

If you plan to grow only a few plants in small containers, the simplest procedure is to buy one of the ready-made mixtures. But for larger plants needing more nutrient solution, buying the chemicals separately and mixing your own will be more economical. Garden supply stores in many areas have one or two mixtures that hobbyists are finding adequate. The following mixture is suitable for most vegetables and flowers.

| | |
|---|---|
| Monobasic potassium phosphate | .5 ounce |
| Potassium nitrate | 2.0 ounces |
| Calcium nitrate | 3.0 ounces |
| Magnesium sulfate (epsom salts) | 1.5 ounces |
| Iron sulfate | 1 teaspoon |
| Water | 25 gallons |

These concentrations are generally suitable during the warm, sunny weather of late spring, summer, and early fall. During late fall and early spring double the amounts of each chemical. During the short, cloudy days of winter, amounts of each concentration should be tripled.

The pH of the nutrient solution should be between 5.5 and 6.5. The mixture given above will have the proper pH when it is first mixed but may change as plants use varying amounts of each chemical from the solution. Test kits are available for checking pH. But the simplest procedure is to change the solution every few days. With the sand-culture method, trouble with pH is less likely, especially if the root medium is occasionally flushed with clear water.

Some high-analysis, agricultural-grade fertilizers are soluble enough to be used in nutrient solutions. These may contain enough impurities to furnish all or part of the trace minerals needed, especially where plants are grown in gravel or cinders that also contain some of the trace minerals. However, some fertilizer grades of phosphate may contain more than 1% fluorine; do not use these in the nutrient solution.

No one nutrient solution is best for all conditions and crops. The following mixture makes use of some of the agricultural grade fertilizers.

Your druggist may be able to weigh out these small amounts for you. Or, to simplify weighing, you can make a concentrated stock solution with 10 times the amount of each in a small quantity of water (5 gallons). This 5 gallons of stock solution is enough to make 1,000 gallons of regular strength. So for 100 gallons of regular strength use ½ gallon of the stock solution;

| | *Amount for 100 Gallons of Water* | |
|---|---|---|
| **MAJOR NUTRIENTS** | | |
| Magnesium sulfate (epsom salts) | 3.2 | ounces |
| Monocalcium phosphate (good grade) | 3.2 | ounces |
| Potassium nitrate | 6.4 | ounces |
| Ammonium sulfate | 1.6 | ounces |
| Calcium sulfate (agricultural gypsum) | 20.8 | ounces |
| **TRACE NUTRIENTS** | | |
| Iron sulfate (copperas) | .4 | ounce |
| Manganese sulfate | .04 | ounce |
| Copper sulfate (blue vitriol) | .013 | ounce |
| Zinc sulfate (zinc vitriol) | .013 | ounce |
| Sodium tetroborate (borax) | .3 | ounce |

for 50 gallons, use 1 quart; for 25 gallons, use 1 pint.

Even when the amount of each nutrient is multiplied by 10, you'll note that only 0.13 ounce each of copper and zinc sulfate will be needed. If your scales will not weigh less then 1 ounce, weigh 1 ounce, and place it on a clean sheet of paper. Then, since 0.13 ounce is about ⅛ ounce, separate the salt into eight piles of as nearly equal size as possible. This can be done by using a knife blade to cut the pile first into halves, then into fourths, then into eighths. Use of one of the eight sections is accurate enough.

Hydroponics is a fascinating hobby, but success is based on a rather exact science. You may encounter some of these difficulties, especially with the water-culture method: keeping the solution at the proper pH, keeping iron in solution, providing proper aeration, keeping the solution at proper concentration, avoiding poor sunlight, and providing proper humidity.

# Organic Vegetable Gardening

Organic gardening consists of using only organic materials (as opposed to synthetic chemical materials) in the vegetable garden. The two areas of gardening in which a real discrepancy exists between organic and nonorganic methods are fertilizers and pest control.

An over-simplified example of what organic gardening is could be found in the methods used 50 years ago or more, before the advent of chemical fertilizers and pesticides. In times past, manure and compost were the only fertilizers available. The only insecticides available were rotenone (made from the root of the derris plant (*Derris eliptica*), pyrethrum (derived from certain plants of the genus *Chrysanthemum*), and nicotine. Companion planting was employed to discourage insects, especially those carrying fungus diseases. Herbicides (weed killers) were unheard of.

Modern organic gardeners object to the use of synthetic chemicals in the garden because of potential residual effects and the destruction of beneficial insects as well as destructive ones. Many organic gardeners, who are sincere naturalists, simply prefer using natural substances rather than chemicals. Most organic gardeners also feel that vegetables grown by organic techniques are tastier and more nutritious than those grown by nonorganic techniques.

One of the greatest contributions of modern organic horticulture has been the breeding of vegetable varieties that are resistant to insects and diseases. Planting resistant varieties is a tremendous advantage for all gardeners, whether their techniques are organic or not.

## Organic Fertilizers

Manure, cottonseed meal, bone meal, alfalfa meal, and others are organic fertilizers, made from derivatives of organic matter, such as animal or plant waste. Organic fertilizers are usually labeled by name (bone meal), while chemical fertilizers are labeled according to chemical analysis (10-6-4).

Manures are effective fertilizers in spite of their mildness. They make the soil more porous and crumbly and improve drainage and aeration. The major disadvantages of organic fertilizers are their increasing cost and their de-creasing availability.

Never add fresh manure to the garden as the level of soluble nitrogen will be too strong for plants. Compost manure with leaves, grass clippings, or the like, or buy dehydrated manure at the garden supply store. Manure that is only partially composted may contain weed seed.

The NPK (nitrogen, phosphorus, potassium) percentages are usually low, around 1-1-1 or 2-1-2. If you compost fresh manure yourself, the NPK percentages may be somewhat greater.

|                 | N      | P     | K   |
|-----------------|--------|-------|-----|
| Poultry manure  | 4–12%  | 2.5%  | 1%  |
| Cattle manure   | 2%     | 1.5%  | 1%  |
| Rabbit manure   | 3%     | 2%    | 1%  |

Other complete organic fertilizers are generally available and widely used:

|                          | N      | P       | K    |
|--------------------------|--------|---------|------|
| Dried blood              | 13%    | 2%      | 1%   |
| Cottonseed meal          | 7%     | 2.5%    | 2%   |
| Fish scrap               | 6%     | 12%     | 4%   |
| Sewage sludge (activated)| 5%     | 4%      | 1%   |
| Castor pomace            | 5%     | 2%      | 1%   |
| Blood meal               | 7–15%  | 1%      | .5%  |
| Soybean meal             | 6–8%   | 1%      | 2%   |
| Linseed meal             | 5%     | 2%      | 2%   |
| Bone meal                | 4%     | 15–24%  | .1%  |

## Green Manure Cover Crops

Another means of fertilizing the vegetable garden and improving soil at the same time is to plant green manure cover crops. These are simply plants that are grown for the sole purpose of plowing them into the soil and thereby enriching the soil with decomposing plant materials. Fall and winter are ideal times to grow cover crops. The cover crop can then be cut and left on the surface to decompose, then tilled into the surface a month or so in advance of spring planting.

The following chart will help you in selecting, planting, and harvesting a green manure cover crop.

Onions are often interplanted with other crops to repell insects and rodents.

## Organic Pest Control

Organic pest control begins with proper variety selection and good cultural practices: thorough soil preparation, adequate fertilization, and mulching to control weeds and conserve moisture. Healthy plants grown in fertile, well-drained soil are less prone to insect and disease attack than weak, struggling plants growing in poor soil.

Companion planting is an important part of insect and nematode control. This technique consists of arranging plants together that are known to grow well together and of interplanting with plants that seem to repel insects.

The primary organic method of controlling insects in the garden is to pick insects off plants by hand and destroy them. The key to insect control is vigilance. Inspect plants *daily* for evidence of insect damage, and remove or destroy them before the infestation has a chance to become rampant.

## Companion Planting

Many plants have an affinity for each other and grow well together. Other plants grow poorly together. All the scientific reasons have not yet been determined, but centuries of human agricultural experience suggest that bush beans, for example, grow well near beets, but that pole beans seem to be inhibited by beets.

Mixed planting can also save space. The following are a few suggestions:

- Pole beans grow well with corn; the cornstalks provide support for the beans as stakes would. Beans are legumes, and all legumes have nitrogen-fixing nodules on their roots that make legumes nitrogen producers rather than nitrogen consumers. Corn needs a lot of nitrogen, so the two plants are mutually beneficial.
- Cabbage and other members of the cabbage family (kohlrabi, cauliflower, broccoli, kale, Brussels sprouts) grow well with onions, garlic, and shallots. Cabbage dislikes strawberries and tomatoes.
- Lettuce grows well with carrots, radishes, onions, beets, and cabbage. Lettuce also grows well near strawberries and could serve as a buffer zone between cabbage and strawberries.
- Peas are compatible in the garden with carrots, cucumbers, radishes, beans, sweet corn, and turnips, but they do not like onions, garlic, and shallots. Do not plant

Castor bean, also called mole plant, is said to repell moles and other small rodents.

# Green Manure Cover Crops

| Common Name | Legume | Soil Preference | Lime Requirements (Low, Medium or Hi. Adapted to Soils of Low Fertility) | Relative Longevity of Seed | Seeding Rate (Pounds per acre) | Seeding Rate (Pounds per 1000 sq. ft.) | Depth to Cover Seed (In.) | N.E. & N.C. States | Southern & S.E. States | Gulf Coast & Florida | Northwestern & Florida | Southwestern States (Areas For Which Best Adapted) | When to Sow | When to Turn Under | Comments |
|---|---|---|---|---|---|---|---|---|---|---|---|---|---|---|---|
| Barley | No | Loams | L | Long | 100 | 2½ | ¾ | • | | | • | Spring / Fall | Summer / Spring | | Not good on sandy or acid soils. Sow spring varieties in north, winter varieties in milder climates. |
| Beans Mung | Yes | Widely Adaptable | L • | Short | 70 | 2 | 1 | | | • | • | Spring or Summer | Summer or Fall | Warm weather crops. Do not sow until ground is warm and weather is settled. |
| Beans Soy | Yes | Loams | M | Short | 90 | 2½ | 1½ | | | • | • | Spring or Summer | Summer or Fall | |
| Beans Velvet | Yes | Loams | L | Short | 120 | 4 | 2 | | | • | • | Spring or Summer | Summer or Fall | |
| Beggar Weed | Yes | Sandy Loams | L • | | 15 | ½ | ½ | | • | | | Spring or Early Summer | Summer or Fall | Seeding rate is for scarified seed. Treble the amount if unhulled seed is used. |
| Brome Grass, Field | No | Widely Adaptable | L | Long | 30 | 1 | ½ | • | | | | Fall / Spring | Spring / Fall | Good winter cover. Easy to establish. Hardier than rye; more heat tolerant. |
| Buckwheat | No | Widely Adaptable | L • | | 50 | 1½ | ¾ | • | | • | | Late Spring and Summer | Summer or Fall | Quick growing. Plant only after ground is warm. |
| Bur Clover | Yes | Heavy Loams | M | Long | 30 | 1 | ½ | | | • | | Fall | Spring | Not winter hardy north. One of the best winter crops where mild winters prevail. |
| Chess or Cheat Grass | No | Loams | L | Long | 40 | 1 | ¾ | • | | | | Fall | Spring | Less sensitive to soil acidity and poorly drained soils than most clovers. |
| Clover Alsike | Yes | Heavy Loams | M • | Long | 8 | ¼ | ½ | • | | | | Spring / Fall | Fall / Spring | |
| Clover Crimson | Yes | Loams | M | Medium | 30 | 1 | ½ | | • | • | | Fall / Spring / Fall | Spring / Fall / Spring | Not winter hardy north. A good winter annual from New Jersey southward. |
| Clover Subterranean | Yes | Loams | M | Medium | 30 | 1 | ½ | | | | | | | |
| Corn | No | Widely Adaptable | L | Medium | 90 | 2½ | 1 | • | | | | Spring or Summer | Summer or Fall | Do not sow until ground is warm. |
| Cow-Pea | Yes | Sandy Loams | L • | Short | 90 | 2½ | 1½ | | • | • | | Late Spring or Early Summer | Summer or Fall | Withstands drought and moderate shade well. Do not sow until weather is warm and settled. |
| Crotalaria | Yes | Light Loams | L | Long | 15 | ½ | ¾ | | • | | | Spring or Summer | Summer or Fall | Does well on acid soils. Resistant to root knot nematode. Sow scarified seed. |
| Fenugreek | Yes | Loams | L | Long | 35 | 1 | ½ | • | | | | Fall | Spring | |
| Guar | Yes | Widely Adaptable | L • | Long | 40 | 1½ | 1 | | • | | | Spring or Early Summer | Summer or Fall | Thrives on warm soils. Do not plant too early. |
| Indigo, Hairy | Yes | Sandy Loams | L • | Short | 10 | ½ | ½ | | • | | | Spring or Early Summer | Summer or Fall | |
| Kale, Scotch | No | Widely Adaptable | H • | Long | 14 | ¼ | ½ | • | | | | Summer or Fall | Spring | Can be eaten after serving as winter cover. In Northern areas interplant with winter rye for protection. Except in deep south, plant in summer for good growth before frost. |
| Lespedeza Common | Yes | Loams | L • | Short | 25 | 1 | ½ | • | | | | Early Spring | Summer or Fall | Easy to establish on hard, badly eroded soils. } Good on acid soils of low fertility. |
| Lespedeza Korean | Yes | Loams | L • | Short | 25 | 1 | ½ | • | | | | Early Spring | Summer or Fall | |
| Lespedeza Sericea | Yes | Loams | L | Medium | 25 | 1 | ½ | • | | | | Early Spring | Summer or Fall | |
| Lupine Blue | Yes | Sandy Loams | L | Short | 100 | 2½ | 1 | | | • | | Spring / Fall | Summer / Spring | Less popular than the yellow lupine and blue lupine. } Good on sour and acid soils. |
| Lupine White | Yes | Sandy Loams | L | Short | 120 | 2½ | 1 | | • | | | Spring | Summer | |
| Lupine Yellow | Yes | Sandy Loams | L | Short | 80 | 2 | 1 | | | • | | Spring / Fall | Summer / Spring | |

| Crop | Inoc. | Soil | | | Growth | Rate | | | Sowing (col A) | Sowing (col B) | Remarks |
|---|---|---|---|---|---|---|---|---|---|---|---|
| Millet | No | Sandy Loams | L | | Long | 30 | 1 | ½ | Late Spring or Summer | Summer or Fall | Sow only after ground is warm, a week or ten days after normal corn planting time. Fast growing. |
| Mustard, White | No | Loams | | | | 8 | ¼ | ¼ | Spring | Summer | |
| Oats | No | Widely Adaptable | L | | Long | 100 | 2½ | 1 | Spring / Fall | Summer or Fall / Spring | Winter oats (sown in fall) are suitable only where mild winters prevail. |
| Pea — Field | Yes | Heavy Loams | M | | Short | 90 | 2½ | 1½ | Early Spring / Fall | Summer / Spring | Sow in fall only where winters are mild. Distinctly a cool weather crop. |
| Pea — Rough | Yes | Sandy Loams | L | • | Medium | 60 | 1½ | 1 | Fall | Spring | |
| Pea — Tangier | Yes | | M | | Medium | 80 | 2½ | 1 | Spring | Summer | |
| Rape | No | Loams | L | | | 8 | ¼ | ¼ | Spring | Summer or Fall | |
| Rescue Grass | No | Widely Adaptable | L | | Long | 35 | 1 | ¾ | Spring or Summer | Summer or Fall | Adapted to mild winters and humid climates. |
| Rye, Spring | No | Widely Adaptable | L | | Long | 90 | 2 | ¾ | Spring | Summer | One of the most important winter cover crops. Can be sown late. |
| Rye, Winter | No | Widely Adaptable | L | | Long | 90 | 2 | ¾ | Fall | Spring | |
| Rye Grass, Italian | No | Widely Adaptable | L | | Long | 35 | 1 | ¾ | Fall / Spring | Spring / Summer | An important winter cover crop where winters are mild. In severe climates sow in spring or summer. |
| Sesbania | Yes | Widely Adaptable | L | • | Long | 25 | 1 | ¾ | Spring or Summer | Summer or Fall | Quick grower. Is better adapted to wet soils and will grow at higher altitudes than crotalaria. |
| Sorghum | No | Light Loams | | | Long | 90 | 2½ | ¾ | Late Spring or Summer | Summer or Fall | Do not sow until ground is warm and weather is settled. More drought resistant than corn. |
| Sudan Grass | No | Widely Adaptable | L | | Long | 35 | 1 | ¾ | Late Spring or Summer | Summer or Fall | Rapid grower. Do not sow until ground is warm and weather is settled. |
| Sunflower | No | Widely Adaptable | L | | | 20 | ¾ | ¾ | Spring or Summer | Summer or Fall | Intolerant of acid soils. |
| Sweet-Clover — Common White | Yes | Heavy Loams | H | | Long | 15 | ½ | ½ | Spring / Fall | | Quite winter hardy. Best results are from fall sowing. |
| Sweet-Clover — Annual (Hubam) | Yes | Loams | H | | Long | 15 | ½ | ½ | Spring / Fall | | A true annual. Best results from spring sowings. |
| Sweet-Clover — Yellow | Yes | Loams | H | | Long | 15 | ½ | ½ | Spring / Fall | | Stands dry conditions better than common white sweet clover. |
| Sweet-Clover — Yellow Annual | Yes | Loams | H | | Long | 15 | ½ | ½ | Spring / Fall | | Most useful south of the cotton belt as winter cover. North not winter hardy. Makes short summer growth. |
| Vetch — Common | Yes | Widely Adaptable | L | | Medium | 60 | 1½ | ¾ | Spring / Fall | Fall / Spring | Not winter hardy where severe cold is experienced. Needs reasonably fertile soil. |
| Vetch — Hairy | Yes | Widely Adaptable | L | | Long | 60 | 1½ | ¾ | Spring / Fall | Fall / Spring | The most winter hardy vetch. Best sown in fall mixed with winter rye or winter wheat. |
| Vetch — Hungarian | Yes | Heavy Loams | L | | Long | 60 | 1½ | ¾ | Spring / Fall | Fall / Spring | Next to hairy vetch the most winter hardy of the vetches. Not winter hardy where winters are severe. |
| Vetch — Purple | Yes | Loams | L | | Long | 60 | 1½ | ¾ | Spring / Fall | Fall / Spring | Needs fairly fertile soil. Least hardy of the vetches. |
| Vetch — Woolly Pod | Yes | Widely Adaptable | L | | Long | 60 | 1½ | ¾ | Spring / Fall | Fall / Spring | Suited for winter cover in mild climates only. |

*Organic Vegetable Gardening*

peas in the same place 2 consecutive years.

- Potatoes grow well with beans, sweet corn, cabbage, and peas. The peas and beans (both legumes) furnish small amounts of nitrogen for the potatoes, while the potatoes help repel the Mexican bean beetle.
- Radishes are said to make lettuce tender. They also repel the striped cucumber beetle.

Some plants have been used for centuries as natural repellents against insects and other garden pests. Nasturtiums, marigolds, garlic, and many herbs have their place in the vegetable garden. Organic gardeners will want to try some of these combinations:

- French Marigolds, planted near tomatoes and other susceptible plants, will help control nematodes and white flies. Planted near snap beans and lima beans, they will serve to ward off bean beetles.
- Nasturtiums are effective against aphids on broccoli and on apples. They also repel squash bugs and white flies.
- Garlic, planted in the garden, wards off moles and other small rodents. Garlic is also beneficial for roses. Garlic tea (a mixture of 1 teaspoon garlic powder to 1 gallon of warm water) is an effective spray for controlling late blight on tomatoes.
- Hyssop increases the yield of grapevines.
- Spearmint repels mosquitoes, ants (plant near porches, terraces, and doorways), black flea beetles, cabbageworm butterflies, and clothes moths.
- Sassafras repels mosquitoes.
- Onions repel rabbits and other rodents. Plant in garden borders with marigolds. Rabbits will not pass through a wall of onions.
- Radishes help repel the striped cucumber beetle.
- Rosemary is offensive to carrotworm butterflies.
- Tansy repels flies, ants, and moths. Planted near peach trees, tansy helps protect them against flying insects.

## Beneficial Insects and Predators

Ladybugs, praying mantids, wasps, birds, and other creatures devour destructive garden insects but do not harm garden plants. A number of these are probably already present in your garden. Learn to recognize beneficial insects, and do not destroy them.

Birds can be both a blessing and a vexation. They eat destructive insects, but they also eat

French marigolds are said to lure nematodes away from susceptible plants such as tomatoes.

beneficial ones. Worse, they eat seed of vegetable plants. (For more information on bird control see Chapter Five, "Controlling Garden Pests.")

### BENEFICIAL INSECTS
#### ASSASSIN BUG
1 to ½ inches long. Feeds on aphids, leafhoppers, and caterpillars.

#### ANT LION
Also called "doodle bug." Traps ants and other insects in a funnel-shaped pit it makes in dry sand.

#### GREEN LACEWING
Yellow green color. Delicate, lacelike wings. Feeds on aphids, mealybugs, and small insects and their eggs.

#### GROUND BEETLE
Feeds at night on caterpillars and their pupae, white grubs, other soft-bodied insects.

## SYRPHID FLY LARVA

Looks and acts like a wasp or bee. Important aphid predator.

## BRACNOID WASP PUPAE

Parasite on caterpillar's skin. Controls hornworms.

## LADY BEETLE

Also called "lacy bug." Preys on aphids, scale insects, and whiteflies.

## STINKBUG

Flattened, shield-shaped. Feeds on caterpillars and beetle larvae.

## PRAYING MANTID

Slender, long-legged, green or brown. Feeds on aphids, leafhoppers, flies, spiders, wasps, bees, beetles.

---

Many beneficial insects can be obtained through commercial sources. Where to buy beneficial insects and nontoxic insecticides:

Insect Biological Control:

- TRIK-O (trade name for Trichogramma wasps)—Gothard, Inc., P.O. Box 370, Canutillo, Tx. 79835. (Recommended for flower and vegetable gardens, berries, grapes, fruit and nut trees, and many field crops; controls apple coddling moth worm)
- Vitova Insectary, Inc., P.O. Box 475, Rialto, Ca. 92376. (Lace-wings and Trichogramma wasps and fly control parasites)
- Eastern Biological Control Co., Route 5, Box 379, Jackson, N.J. 08527. (Trichogramma wasps)
- LADYBUGS—Bio-Control Company, Route 2, Box 2397, Auburn, Ca. 95603.
- L. E. Schooner, Rough & Ready, Ca. 95975; Montgomery Ward, 618 W. Chicago Avenue, Chicago, Ill. 60610.
- PRAYING MANTIDS—Eastern Biological Control Co., Route 5, Box 379, Jackson, N.J. 08527; Montgomery Ward, 618 W. Chicago Avenue, Chicago, Ill. 60610.

Insect Disease Control:

- "DOOM" (milky disease spores control Japanese beetle grubs and other grubs)—Fairfax Biological Laboratory, Clinton Corners, N.Y. 12514.

## ORGANIC INSECTICIDES

Rotenone and pyrethrum are two of the oldest and most reliable insecticides available. Garlic tea can be effective in repelling insects but not in destroying them. Slugs and snails can be controlled by setting tiny saucers of beer near damaged plants; these insects come out at night, drink the beer, and drown in it.

To control slugs and snails, set a shallow saucer or piepan of beer near slug-damaged plants in the evening. Hollow out enough soil to allow the rim of the pan to set flush with the soil. Slugs and snails are lured to the beer, then drown in it.

# Fall and Winter Gardening in the South

Growing vegetables in most of the South can be a year-round project. The fall, winter, and early spring are the times to grow such cool-season vegetables as cabbage, cauliflower, broccoli, greens, and English peas. The use of hotbeds and cold frames extends the list of winter vegetables and allows you to start spring vegetables early.

### September

- Begin to get the garden ready for early fall plantings of greens and salad crops. Mix fertilizer and organic matter into soil, and prepare to plant.
- If nematodes have been a problem in your garden treat infected areas with an approved nematocide or fumigate with methyl bromide. Follow package directions for amounts to use and for method of application.
- Plant beets, carrots, chard, kale, lettuce, mustard, onions (seed or sets), radishes,

Carrots can be grown throughout the winter in much of the South.

and turnips. Try several different kinds of lettuce—butterhead, romaine, and green or bronze leaf.
- For best germination of lettuce and other small seed, keep the soil moist and cool with daily sprinklings.

### October

- October also is a good month for planting cool-season vegetable crops such as turnips, mustard, kale, spinach, lettuce, and radishes. Also, set out young plants of onion and cabbage.
- Green tomatoes that have insufficient time to ripen before frost can be brought indoors to ripen gradually.
- Harvest gourds and pumpkins when the skins get hard.

### November

- Try to gather all warm-weather crops before the first killing frost. Pick green tomatoes, and place them in a warm, sunny window to ripen. In the Lower South, plant seed of beets, carrots, kale, lettuce, peas,

Turnips are a popular cool-season crop. They are grown for the greens in the South and for the edible enlarged root in the North.

Cabbage is an excellent cool-season crop, rich in nutrients and flavor.

Broccoli, a member of the cabbage family, is a cool-season vegetable for the fall or early spring garden.

Cauliflower, like broccoli and other members of the cabbage family, likes cool weather and should be planted in the fall garden or in early spring.

Baby or green onions can be used as a seasoning. Onions in general grow best in cool weather.

radishes, and turnips. Already-started plants of cabbage, broccoli, Brussels sprouts, and cauliflower should be set out now.

- Cut and dispose of asparagus tops as soon as the frost has killed them.

## December

- Parsnips, salsify (oyster plant), turnips, carrots, and other root crops may be left in their rows in the garden and pulled as they are needed.
- Apply 4 to 6 inches of mulch to protect cabbage, collards, and other hardy vegetables.
- Prepare hotbeds and cold frames for growing hardy vegetables and for growing plants that will be set out when the warm spring weather arrives.
- In the Lower South plant English peas, lettuce, spinach, and onion sets.

## January

- Seed of hardy vegetables such as beets, collards, mustard, turnips, Chinese cabbage, lettuce, carrots, spinach, radishes, and peas may be planted this month in the Lower South. Set out onion, cabbage, and asparagus plants. These plantings must be delayed until February in the Middle South and until March in the Upper South.
- Seed of tomato, eggplant, and pepper may be sown now in hotbeds and transplanted next month into cold frames.

- If you are planning a vegetable garden for the first time or if you are relocating, choose a sunny, well-drained location that is far enough removed from trees and shrubs to avoid competition with their roots for the nutrients in the soil. Spread 3 or 4 inches of organic matter (peat moss, well-rotted manure, old leaves, compost, if you have it) over the entire plot, and either till or hoe this into the soil.
- In the Middle and Lower South, there is still time to plant the following cool-season vegetables: beets, collards, mustard, turnips, Chinese cabbage, lettuce, carrots, spinach, radishes, Swiss chard, and English peas.
- Set out plants of onion, cabbage, asparagus, and Brussels sprouts.
- Seeds for indoor sowing now include peppers, tomatoes, eggplant, and broccoli. When warm weather arrives, these plants should be large enough to set outdoors.

## February

- In the Middle and Lower South, there is still time to plant beets, collards, mustard, turnips, Chinese cabbage, lettuce, carrots, spinach, radishes, Swiss chard, and English peas.
- Set out plants of onion, cabbage, asparagus, horseradish, and Brussels sprouts.
- Seeds for indoor sowing now include peppers, tomatoes, eggplant, and broccoli. When warm weather arrives, these plants should be large enough to set outdoors.

# Appendix

COOPERATIVE EXTENSION SERVICES IN THE 50 STATES

**ALABAMA**
Cooperative Extension Service
Auburn University
Auburn, Alabama 36830

**ALASKA**
Cooperative Extension Service
University of Alaska
College, Alaska 99701

**ARIZONA**
Cooperative Extension Service
University of Arizona
College of Agriculture
Tucson, Arizona 85721

**ARKANSAS**
Agricultural Extension Service
University of Arkansas
P.O. Box 391
Little Rock, Arkansas 72203

**CALIFORNIA**
Cooperative Extension Service
University of California
College of Agriculture
Berkeley, California 94720

**COLORADO**
Cooperative Extension Service
Colorado State University
Fort Collins, Colorado 80521

**CONNECTICUT**
Cooperative Extension Service
University of Connecticut
College of Agriculture and
   Natural Resources
Storrs, Connecticut 06268

**DELAWARE**
Cooperative Extension Service
University of Delaware
College of Agricultural Sciences
Newark, Delaware 19711

**FLORIDA**
Agricultural Extension Service
University of Florida
Institute of Food and Agricul-
   tural Sciences
Gainesville, Florida 32601

**GEORGIA**
Cooperative Extension Service
University of Georgia
College of Agriculture
Athens, Georgia 30601

**HAWAII**
Cooperative Extension Service
College of Tropical Agriculture
Honolulu, Hawaii 96822

**IDAHO**
Cooperative Extension Service
University of Idaho
College of Agriculture
Moscow, Idaho 83843

**ILLINOIS**
Cooperative Extension Service
University of Illinois
College of Agriculture
Urbana, Illinois 61801

**INDIANA**
Cooperative Extension Service
Purdue University
Lafayette, Indiana 47907

**IOWA**
Cooperative Extension Service
Iowa State University
Ames, Iowa 50010

**KANSAS**
Cooperative Extension Service
Kansas State University
Manhattan, Kansas 66520

**KENTUCKY**
Cooperative Extension Service
University of Kentucky
College of Agriculture
Lexington, Kentucky 40506

**LOUISIANA**
Cooperative Extension Service
State University A. & M. College
University Station
Baton Rouge, Louisiana 70803

**MAINE**
Cooperative Extension Service
University of Maine
Orono, Maine 04473

**MARYLAND**
Cooperative Extension Service
University of Maryland
College Park, Maryland 20742

**MASSACHUSETTS**
Cooperative Extension Service
University of Massachusetts
Amherst, Massachusetts 01002

**MICHIGAN**
Cooperative Extension Service
Michigan State University
East Lansing, Michigan 48823

**MINNESOTA**
Cooperative Extension Service
University of Minnesota
Institute of Agriculture
St. Paul, Minnesota 55101

**MISSISSIPPI**
Cooperative Extension Service
Mississippi State University
State College, Mississippi 39762

**MISSOURI**
Cooperative Extension Service
University of Missouri
Columbia, Missouri 65201

**MONTANA**
Cooperative Extension Service
Montana State University
Bozeman, Montana 59715

**NEBRASKA**
Cooperative Extension Service
University of Nebraska
College of Agriculture and Home
   Economics
Lincoln, Nebraska 68503

**NEVADA**
Cooperative Extension Service
University of Nevada
College of Agriculture
Reno, Nevada 89507

**NEW HAMPSHIRE**
Cooperative Extension Service
University of New Hampshire
College of Life Sciences and
   Agriculture
Durham, New Hampshire 03824

NEW JERSEY
Cooperative Extension Service
Rutgers University
College of Agriculture and
    Environmental Science
New Brunswick, New Jersey
    08903

NEW MEXICO
Cooperative Extension Service
New Mexico State University
Las Cruces, New Mexico 88001

NEW YORK
Cooperative Extension Service
New York State College of Agri-
    culture and Home Economics
Ithaca, New York 14850

NORTH CAROLINA
Cooperative Extension Service
North Carolina State University
P.O. Box 5157
Raleigh, North Carolina 27607

NORTH DAKOTA
Cooperative Extension Service
North Dakota State University
Agricultural College
Fargo, North Dakota 58102

OHIO
Cooperative Extension Service
Ohio State University
Agricultural Administration
    Building
2120 Fyffe Road
Columbus, Ohio 43210

OKLAHOMA
Cooperative Extension Service
Oklahoma State University
Box 1008
Stillwater, Oklahoma 74074

OREGON
Cooperative Extension Service
Oregon State University
Corvallis, Oregon 97331

PENNSYLVANIA
Agricultural Information
Pennsylvania State University
Room 1, Armsby Building
University Park, Pennsylvania
    16802

RHODE ISLAND
Cooperative Extension Service
University of Rhode Island
Kingston, Rhode Island
    02881

SOUTH CAROLINA
Cooperative Extension Service
Clemson University
Clemson, South Carolina
    29631

SOUTH DAKOTA
Cooperative Extension Service
South Dakota State University
College of Agricultural and
    Biological Sciences
Brookings, South Dakota
    57006

TENNESSEE
Agricultural Extension Service
University of Tennessee
Institute of Agriculture
P.O. Box 1071
Knoxville, Tennessee 37901

TEXAS
Agricultural Extension Service
Texas A & M University
College Station, Texas 77843

UTAH
Cooperative Extension Service
Utah State University
Logan, Utah 84321

VERMONT
Cooperative Extension Service
University of Vermont
Burlington, Vermont 05401

VIRGINIA
Cooperative Extension Service
Virginia Polytechnic Institute
Blacksburg, Virginia 24061

WASHINGTON
Cooperative Extension Service
Washington State University
College of Agriculture
Pullman, Washington 99163

WEST VIRGINIA
Cooperative Extension Service
West Virginia University
Morgantown, West Virginia
    26506

WISCONSIN
Cooperative Extension Service
University of Wisconsin
432 North Lake Street
Madison, Wisconsin 53706

WYOMING
Cooperative Extension Service
University of Wyoming
College of Agriculture
Box 1154
University Station
Laramie, Wyoming 82070

# Glossary

*Annual*—A plant that lives for 1 year.

*Bare-rooted plant*—A plant to be set out that has no soil ball retained about its roots.

*Bolting*—Going to seed prematurely.

*Broadcast*—To scatter fertilizer or other materials over the entire garden area as opposed to specific placing of fertilizer in or along seed rows.

*Cold frame*—A hotbed without heat. *See* Hotbed.

*Compacted soil*—Heavy soil that has been packed or worked when too wet and, therefore, is hard.

*Compost*—A mixture of leaves, plant refuse, garbage, or table scraps partially decayed, prepared, and used for fertilizing or renovating land.

*Cross-fertilization*—A process whereby the pollen from one plant or species or variety is placed on the pistil of a flower of another plant, species, or variety.

*Crown*—1) The top and center of a root system; the junction of stem and root in a seed plant. 2) The leafy section of a tree.

*Cuttings*—The parts of a plant used to start new plants, usually the stems, leaves, or roots.

*Damping-off*—A name covering various fungus diseases affecting seedlings, causing them to rot near soil level. Brought on by overcrowding, excess humidity, poor drainage, and soggy or unsterilized soil. Cheshunt Compound, a chemical, will control the disease.

*Dig in*—To incorporate fertilizer or other materials into the soil during the process of spading.

*Division*—The process of starting new plants by removing a portion of a plant, usually the roots, shoots, or above ground sections; that is, separating daylilies, dividing garlic bulbs into buds, etc.

*Dust*—To apply a dry chemical to a plant.

*Fungicide*—Chemical applied to plant to aid in disease control.

*Furrow*—A trench in the earth made by a plow, hoe, or other implement.

*Harden off*—To prepare a plant for colder or more rigorous conditions by gradually raising or lowering temperatures or by witholding water so that plant can be transferred from indoors to outdoors.

*Hardiness*—Ability of a plant to withstand winter outdoors in a cold climate without protection.

*Hardpan*—A hard layer of soil a few inches under ground level formed as a result of constant shallow plowing.

*Harrow*—To break up the surface of the soil by dragging an implement (containing disks or spikes) made for this purpose.

*Herbicide*—Chemical used to kill weeds.

*Hotbed*—An enclosed structure, with a light-transmitting cover near the ground, in which soil is heated by fermenting material, hot-water pipes, or electric heating cables.

*Hybrid*—A plant resulting from the crossbreeding of two or more plants.

*Insecticides*—Chemicals used to kill insects.

*Larva*—The growing wormlike stage of insects that go through complete metamorphosis. The stages of metamorphosis are egg, larva, pupa, and adult.

*Legume*—The fruit or seed of a leguminous plant such as peas, beans, etc.

*Mosaic*—A disease of a number of different vegetables that distorts growth and is caused by one or more viruses.

*Mulch*—Material applied to the soil surface to conserve moisture and control weeds.

*Nematode*—One of a group of tiny wormlike creatures that damage plants by feeding on or within the roots.

*Organic matter*—A part of the soil resulting from decaying or decayed plant material (humus).

*Peat (Muck)*—Well-rotted, organic matter composed of fine particles.

*Peat moss (Sphagnum moss)*—Coarse, fibrous material that has not decayed.

*Pesticide*—Any chemical or mixture of chemicals used to control plant and animal pests including insects, diseases, weeds, rodents, etc.

*Perennial*—A plant that lives for more than 2 years.

*pH*—(Literally means potential for hydrogen.) A measure of the acidity or alkalinity of the soil, using a 1 to 14 scale with 7 being neutral. Plants generally grow best at a pH of 5.5 to 7.0.

*Plant band*—A small circle or square of paper or other material placed in seed flats to separate young plants and make transplanting easier by retaining a ball of soil with the roots.

*Propagation*—To start new plants from seed, cuttings, or other plant parts.

*Seedbed*—An area in the garden prepared for seeding, usually a row.

*Set*—A young bulb or tuber that is ready for planting.

*Side-dressing*—Application of fertilizer on either side of a seed row or in a circle around a hill planting.

*Spindly*—Abnormally tall and thin.

*Sucker*—A shoot of a bush or tree that arises from below ground level rather than from the stem or trunk.

*Tender plant*—A plant that cannot survive freezing temperatures.

*Transplant*—To lift and reset a plant in another soil or situation.

*Tuber*—A short, thickened underground stem (sometimes applied to thickened underground roots).

*Variety (or Cultivar)*—The subdivision of a species. A group of individuals within a species that are distinct in form or function from other members of the species in certain minor characteristics. These characteristics are usually perpetuated through generations by seed.

# Index

Irish potatoes, 5, 6, 9, 24, 25, 35, 39, 47, 63, 100
  how to grow, 70
Irish potato scab (fungus disease), 48
Irrigation, 32, 35

## J

Japanese beetle, 49, 101
Japanese tomato ring, 78

## K

Kale, 6, 9, 19, 24, 25, 39, 43, 85, 87, 97, 98, 102, 104
  how to grow, 63–64
Kohlrabi, 6, 9, 24, 25, 85, 97
  how to grow, 64

## L

Ladybugs, 100, 101
Lamb's lettuce. *See* Corn salad
Late blight (bacterial disease), 5, 47, 63, 100
Leafhopper, 47, 100, 101
Leaf miners, 48
Leaf spot (fungus disease), 44, 46
Leeks, 24, 25, 67, 87
  how to grow, 68
Legume, 98–99
Lemon balm, 91, 92
Lespedeza, 98
Lettuce, 5, 6, 7, 9, 19, 24, 25, 30, 39, 46, 63, 85, 87, 89, 90, 97, 100, 102, 104
  how to grow, 64–65
Lettuce drop, 46
Lima beans, 6, 9, 24, 25, 35, 36, 43, 100. *See also* Butter beans
Lime, 11, 12, 15, 40, 56, 73, 93, 98, 99
  how to use, 13, 52
Lovage, 82, 92
Lupine, 98

## M

Marigolds, 51, 67, 100
Mealybugs, 69, 100
Melonworm, 44
Mice, 33
Mildew (fungus disease), 5, 40
Millet, 99
Mint, 80, 81, 82
Moles, 33, 97, 100

Mosaic (virus disease), 5, 40, 43, 44, 45, 47, 77
Mosquitoes, 100
Mulch, mulching, 32–34
  materials for, 32, 33
Muskmelons, 24, 25
  how to grow, 65–66
Mustard greens, 5, 6, 9, 24, 25, 39, 43, 85, 87, 99, 102, 104
  how to grow, 66

## N

Nasturtiums, 51, 74, 85, 100
Neck rot (of onions), 46
Nematocide, 42, 67, 77, 102
Nematodes, 30, 40, 41, 42, 43, 44, 46, 47, 51, 55, 57, 67, 69, 70, 75, 77, 89, 91, 97, 100, 102, 107
Nutrient solution, 92, 93
  how to make, 94–95
Nutritional values, 6

## O

Oats, 99
Okra, 5, 6, 24, 25, 35, 39, 40, 46, 84, 85, 86
  how to grow, 66–67
Onions, 5, 6, 9, 19, 24, 25, 30, 39, 46, 63, 70, 85, 87, 90, 97, 100, 102, 103, 104
  how to grow, 67
Oregano, 80, 81, 83, 91, 92
Oyster plant. *See* Salsify

## P

Pansy, 51
Parsley, 24, 25, 80, 81, 83, 88, 91, 92
Parsnips, 24, 25, 39, 71
  how to grow, 68
Patio containers, 69
Peach trees, 100
Peas, English, 5, 6, 9, 24, 25, 36, 39, 47, 55, 85, 90, 97, 100, 102, 104
  how to grow, 68–69
Peas, snow. *See* Peas, English
Peas, Southern, 9, 35, 39, 47
  how to grow, 69
Pentachlorophenol, 28
Peppermint, 80, 82
Peppers, 6, 9, 19, 24, 25, 30, 35, 39, 47, 63, 84, 85, 88, 90, 104
  how to grow, 69–70

Tomatoes, 5, 6, 7, 19, 24, 25, 30, 36, 39, 40, 41, 47, 51, 63, 70, 84, 85, 86, 88, 90, 97, 100, 102, 104
   how to grow, 74–78
Tools, 8
Tortoise beetles, 48
Transplanting, 19, 26, 107
Trellises, 36, 37, 53, 54, 61, 76, 85
Turnips, 5, 6, 7, 9, 24, 25, 39, 43, 71, 85, 88, 97, 102, 104
   how to grow, 78

# V

Vegetable weevils, 49
Vetch, 99

# W

Wasps, 100, 101
Water culture, 95

Watermelons, 5, 6, 24, 25, 39, 40, 44, 55, 84
   how to grow, 79
Weed control, 32, 35–36
White flies, 63, 101
White grubs, 40, 49, 100
White leaf spot (fungus disease), 43
Wilt (bacterial disease), 5, 40, 44, 46, 48, 69, 75
Wireworms, 40, 46, 48, 49

# Y

Yams. *See* Sweet potatoes
Yellows (fungus disease), 5, 44

# Z

Zinnia, 51